A History of Irel[...]

General Editor

Margaret MacCurtain, O.[...]

A History of Ireland

Celts and Normans
Conquest and Colonisation
The Birth of Modern Ireland

Celts and Normans

Gearóid MacGearailt, M.A.

GILL AND MACMILLAN

28910

First Published in 1969

Gill and Macmillan Limited
2 Belvedere Place
Dublin 1

Cover design by Cor Klaasen

Produced in Ireland at The Richview Press Limited.

Contents

Preface

The study of Irish history has always offered that special kind of experience associated with a memorable past that goes back into antiquity. It is an experience that appeals to different kinds of minds. Some enjoy reconstructing the archaeological evidence of ancient Ireland. Others find pleasure in recapturing the life of medieval Ireland with its busy monastery cities and its Viking and Norman settlements. All this is brought to life by narrative and by illustrations in the first volume of *A History of Ireland*. One notable feature is the ease with which the great riches of the Irish manuscript collections of prose and poetry are made available and explained in this first volume.

Interest about the history of colonization in general has given a new direction to the history of conquest and plantation in sixteenth and seventeenth century Ireland. It is an interest linked up with historical geography and with the study of social history. These are main themes in the second volume. The introduction of the Reformation into Ireland, the development of the Irish parliament, and the administering of the great estates of eighteenth century Ireland are treated with an awareness of events in Europe and Britain. There is also an emphasis on local history which many readers will welcome.

To tell the story of Ireland in the nineteenth and twentieth centuries imposes a responsibility of being impartial on both writer and reader. This is particularly true of the recent past. In the third volume, movements in the last century which have shaped the present have been explained with some detail. Wherever possible a sense of immediacy has been created by quoting from a contemporary witness or by an illustration of the period.

A History of Ireland is a joint effort resulting from years of thought about the teaching of history. Each chapter may be used as a single topic, or as a series of projects with reading lists and suggestions for a more detailed approach to the central issue. The writers have brought to their readers the results of their own learning, a learning that is, in turn, the result of much scholarship and research which has been going on quietly in Ireland during the last thirty years.

On many occasions the helpful advice of friends and the generous assistance of many others, each an expert in his own field, have made the compiling of these books a pleasant undertaking. To all we extend a cordial thanks.

Dublin, June 1969 *M. MacCurtain*

The Earliest Inhabitants

Ireland has been inhabited by man for over 8,000 years. Since the first people came, others have been coming, some peaceful, some warlike, down almost to modern times, and all these taken together make up the Irish people. The history of Ireland is the story of all the peoples who lived in Ireland, their way of life, their farms and homes, their cities, their art and literature, their wars and battles.

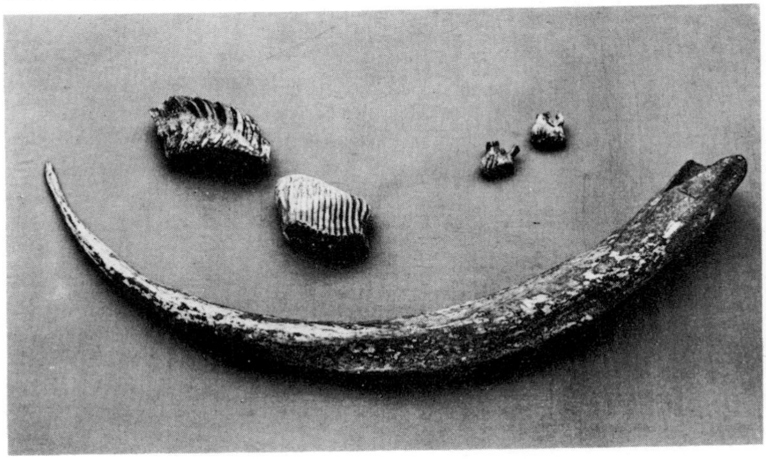

The teeth and tusks of the Mammoth, an extinct variety of elephant, which roamed Ireland long before the coming of man.

Hunters and Fishermen: 6,000–3,500 B.C.

In 6,000 B.C. Ireland was covered with dense forest of pine and hazel, oak and elm. About this time the first people crossed over from Scandinavia to Britain and made their way across the narrow sea from Scotland to Ireland. Because of the thick forests, these people travelled along the rivers and lakes and along the sea-coast. They made their way up the Bann to

The antlers of the Giant Irish deer from Jamestown, Co. Tipperary. This animal had an antler-span of more than nine feet and lived in Ireland about 9500 B.C.

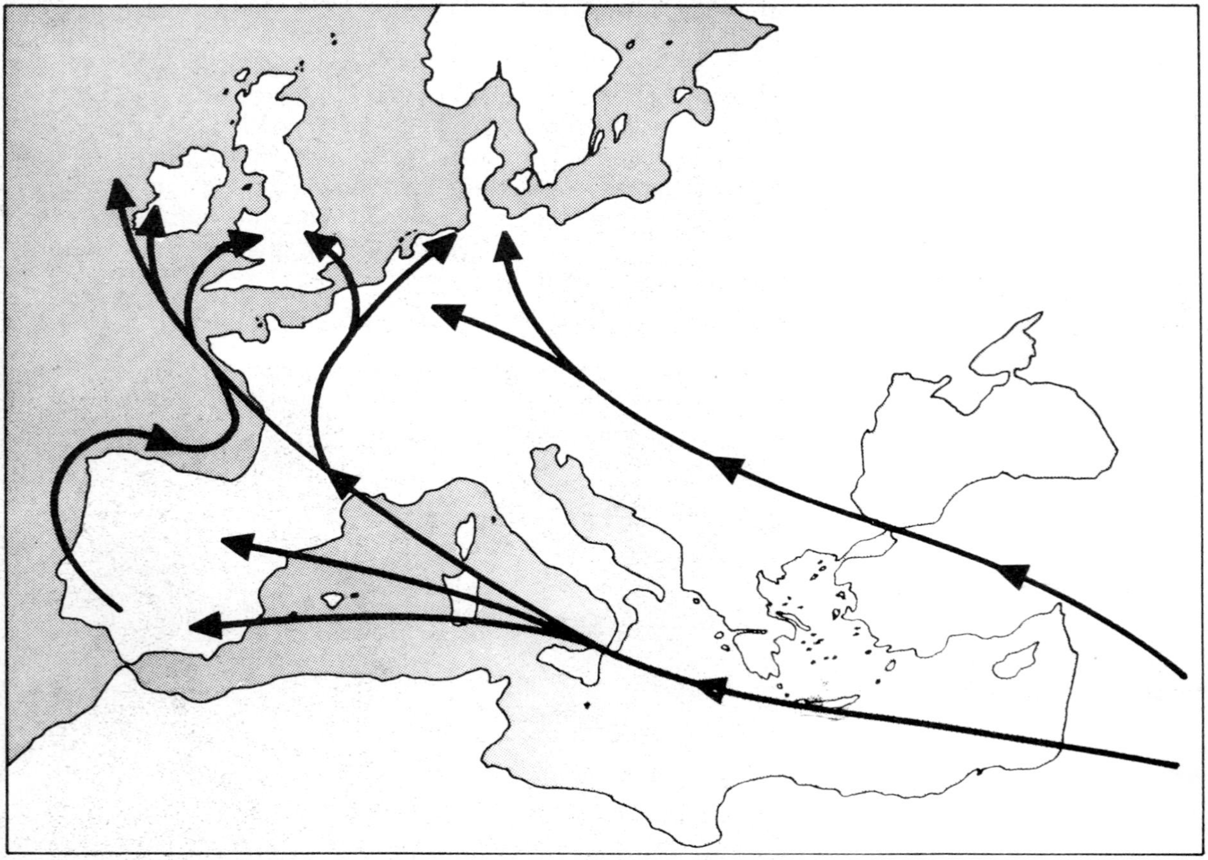

Lough Neagh and spread slowly southwards to Limerick and Carlow. They were hunters and fishermen and lived mostly beside the lakes and rivers. They collected berries and shell-fish and they hunted wild animals. They knew nothing about farming and they lived off the food they gathered and the wild animals which they hunted. Their weapons and tools were made of flint and bone and they had boats of hide like the curraghs you can still see on the west coast of Ireland. Theirs was the first and greatest wave of immigrants and their blood still runs strongly in our veins. According to scholars, they were tall, broad-shouldered and large-chested; their heads were large, their foreheads broad and high; their faces were broad and slightly flattish, the mouth large, with a prominent chin. Their hair was brown and wavy, often red; their eyes light-mixed blue. The skin was typically inclined to freckling, and very fair.

Farming began in the Middle East. This map shows how the first farmers spread westwards along the Danube and along the Mediterranean sea-routes (from about 4000 B.C.).

A decorated stone from the great megalithic tomb at Newgrange, in the Boyne valley.

A stone spiral carved on one of the megaliths of Newgrange.

The great mound of the megalithic tomb at Knowth, in the Boyne valley. This picture shows the diggings of the archaeologists. Around the base of the mound is a great circle of large stones. Beneath this mound lies a great megalithic tomb.

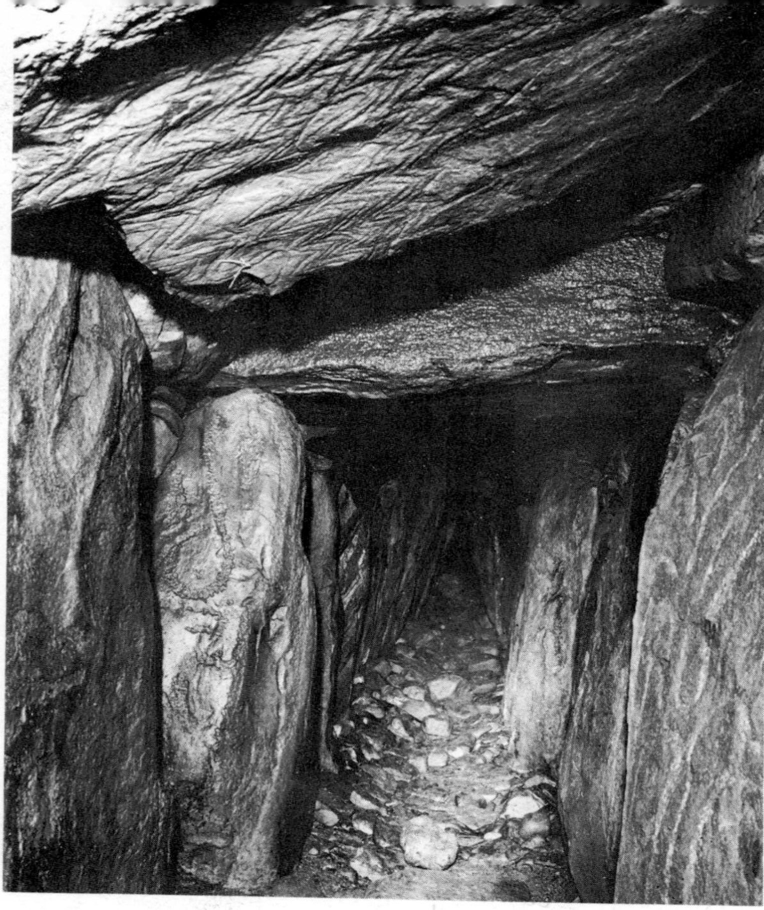

This is a photograph taken inside the megalithic tomb at Knowth. The standing stones support the large stones which form the roof.

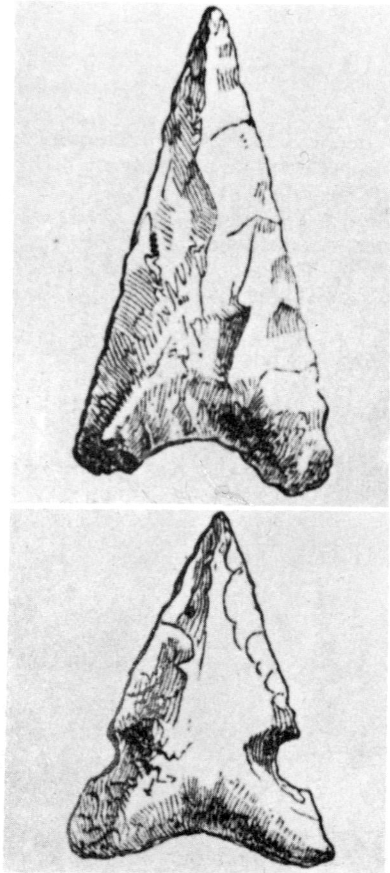

Stone arrow-heads

Farmers and Herdsmen: 3,500–2,000 B.C.

Meanwhile, in the Middle East man made great progress. Men learned how to till the land and grow and harvest grain. They also learned how to keep domestic animals to provide meat, milk and hides. They discovered pottery and learned how to polish stone tools and axes to make them sharp and

A dolmen, another type of megalithic tomb. A dolmen usually consists of three upright stones which support a large flat stone. These stones often weigh many tons.

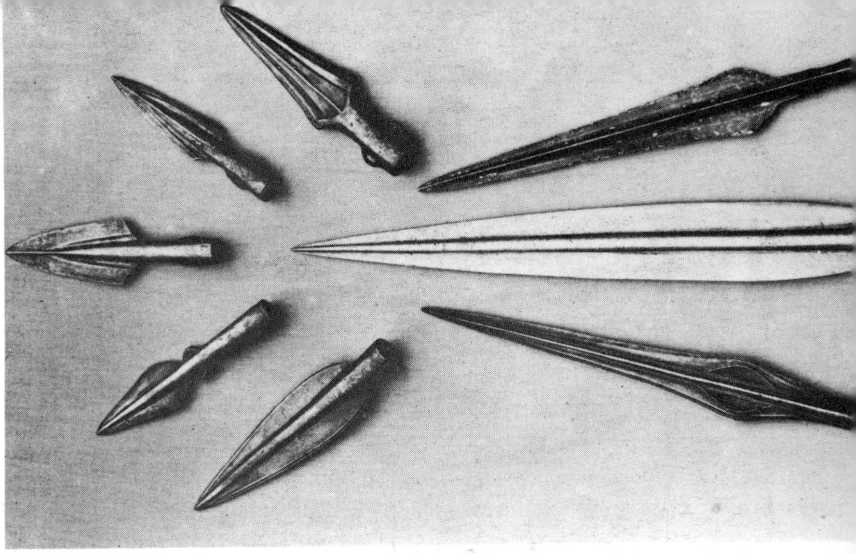

Bronze-age spear-heads. The smaller ones were tied to the shafts. The larger ones were fixed on the shafts with pegs.

Bronze hatchet-heads which date from between 1800 B.C. to about 500 B.C.

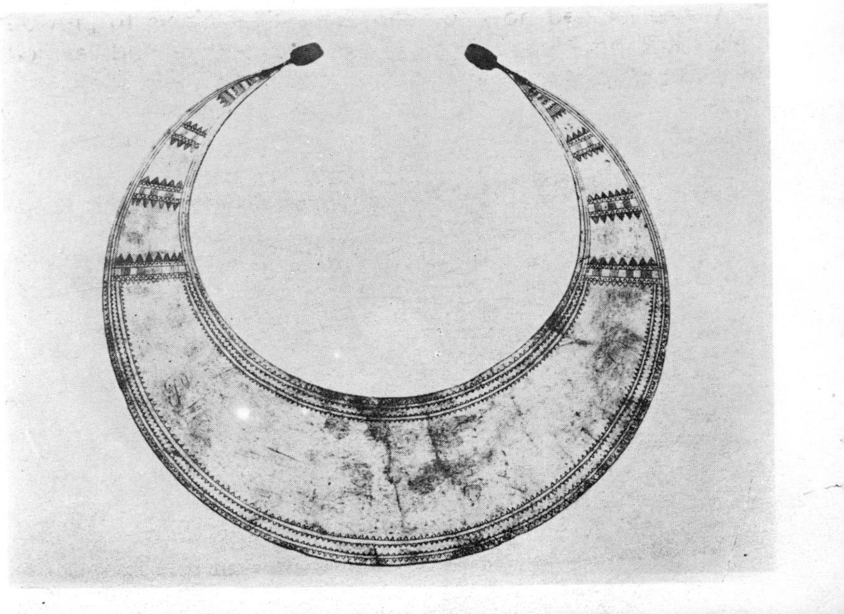

A gold ornament which was probably worn around the neck. It was found at Lough Lee, Co. Westmeath and probably dates from about 1800 B.C.

A shield of beaten bronze which was found near Lough Gur, Co. Limerick. It belongs to the late bronze age and dates from about 700 B.C.

Bronze-age swords and daggers. The rapier in the centre dates from about 1500 B.C. The two daggers date from about 1000 B.C. The swords date from about 750 B.C.

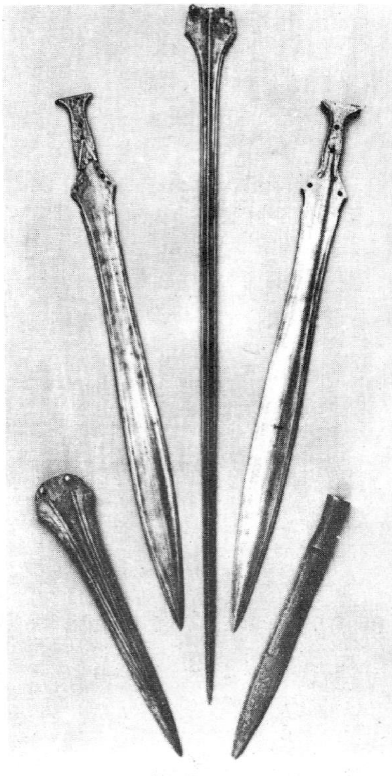

effective. These first farmers set out in search of new lands, spreading slowly westwards and northwards, and the first of them reached Ireland about 3,500 B.C.

In Ireland, they settled on the light limestone lands which were easy to work. They made houses of turves with wooden frames and thatched them with rushes. They used stone axes to cut down the forest and till the ground for corn. They knew how to weave woollen cloth and they had bone needles and awls. They also kept large numbers of cattle, pigs and sheep. These were our first farmers and many of their customs and beliefs lived on until our own time.

Leather was also used to make shields. This is a leather shield, found at Cloonbrin, Co. Longford. It dates from about 700 B.C.

Late bronze age trumpets which date from about 800 B.C.

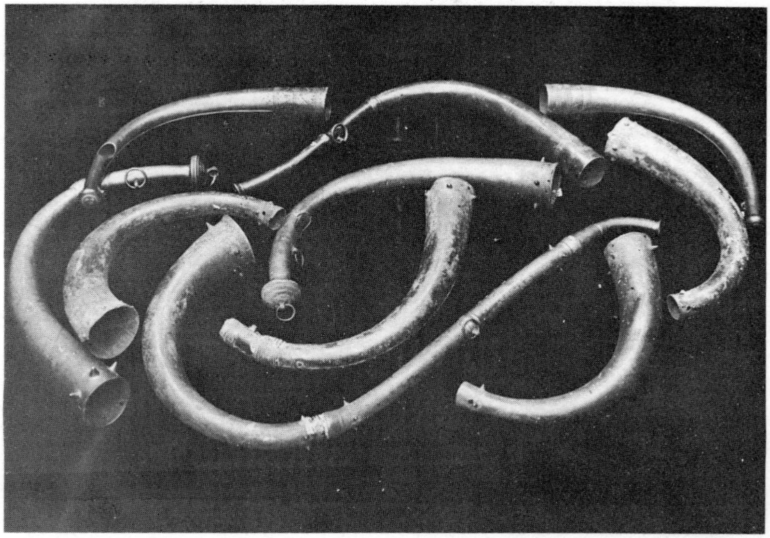

They were a rich and prosperous people. They and other farming peoples who came later built great stone monuments, called megaliths, to the memory of the dead and for religious purposes.

Some of these megaliths contain as much as 12,000 tons of stone, and they decorated the larger stones with wonderful spirals and zig-zag patterns. One of the most famous of the megalithic tombs is at New Grange, on the Boyne, but they are to be found in most parts of Ireland. These people probably believed in a Sun God and an Earth Goddess.

A cauldron or great cooking-pot made of sheets of bronze fastened with rivets. It belongs to about 700 B.C. and it was found at Castlederg, Co. Tyrone.

Bronze Workers and Goldsmiths: 2,000 B.C.

None of the inhabitants of Ireland knew yet about the use of metals. It was in the Middle East that men first learned how to manufacture metal tools, swords and ornaments. About 2,000 B.C. the first metal workers reached Ireland and many of the copper deposits, which they discovered, are still being mined today. In Ireland, they set up a great bronze-working industry. They manufactured bronze axes, tools, cauldrons and ornaments and they exported some of their products to Britain and other countries.

They discovered gold in Wicklow and they made beautiful ornaments, some of which you can see in the National Museum. Another group of invaders and settlers came about 1,200 B.C. bringing new ideas and new weapons and they mixed with the rest of the population. Ireland was peaceful and prosperous in this period; and side by side with her rich agriculture the trade in bronze objects flourished. However, far away in Central Europe another great people was rising to power. These were the Celts, the last and greatest invaders of Ireland in ancient times.

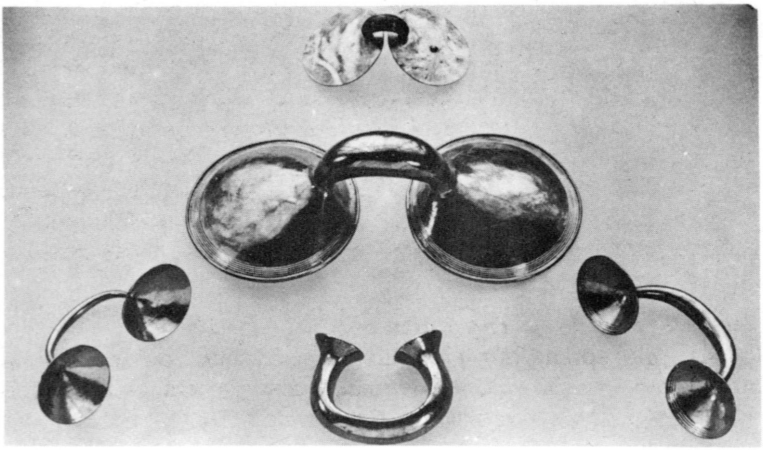

Gold dress-fasteners. Some of them are solid, some hollow. They belong to the late bronze age, after 1000 B.C.

Things to Do

1. Go to the library and ask to see Ó Ríordáin and Daniel, *Newgrange.* Examine the photographs in this book of the great megalithic tomb at Newgrange on the Boyne.
2. Find out if there are any megalithic tombs or dolmens in your area. If there are, write a description of them.

Books to Read or Consult

Victor Skipp, *Out of the Ancient World,* London 1967. This book will tell you a great deal about the early history of man, the great empires, the discovery of writing and agriculture and the spread of ancient peoples.

S. P. Ó Ríordáin, *Antiquities of the Irish countryside,* London 1964.

The Gleninsheen Gorget. It is a gold collar which was made about 650 B.C. It was found in a cleft in the rocks at Gleninsheen, Co. Clare.

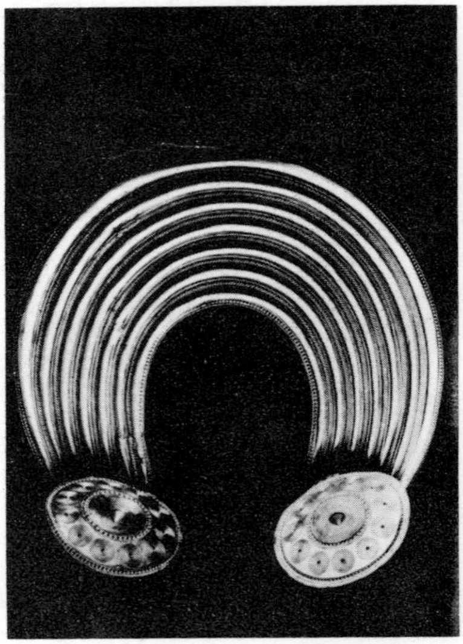

The Celts

The Origin of the Celts

The home of the Celts was east of the Rhine and north of the Alps in the lands now called Bavaria and Bohemia. They were a pastoral and agricultural people with a long and rich tradition and they were greatly influenced by the highly civilized peoples to the south and east of them. The Celts were vigorous and warlike and, from time to time, groups of them led by military chiefs migrated in search of fresh lands and new peoples to conquer. Between 700 and 600 B.C. they became an iron-using people, made up of separate tribes and led by powerful and wealthy kings who were busy conquering central Europe.

The Expansion of the Celts

The Celts spread out in all directions; westwards into France and Spain, northwards into Ireland and Britain, southwards into Italy, and eastwards into Greece and Asia Minor. Before

This map shows the expansion of the Celts from their original homeland in Central Europe.

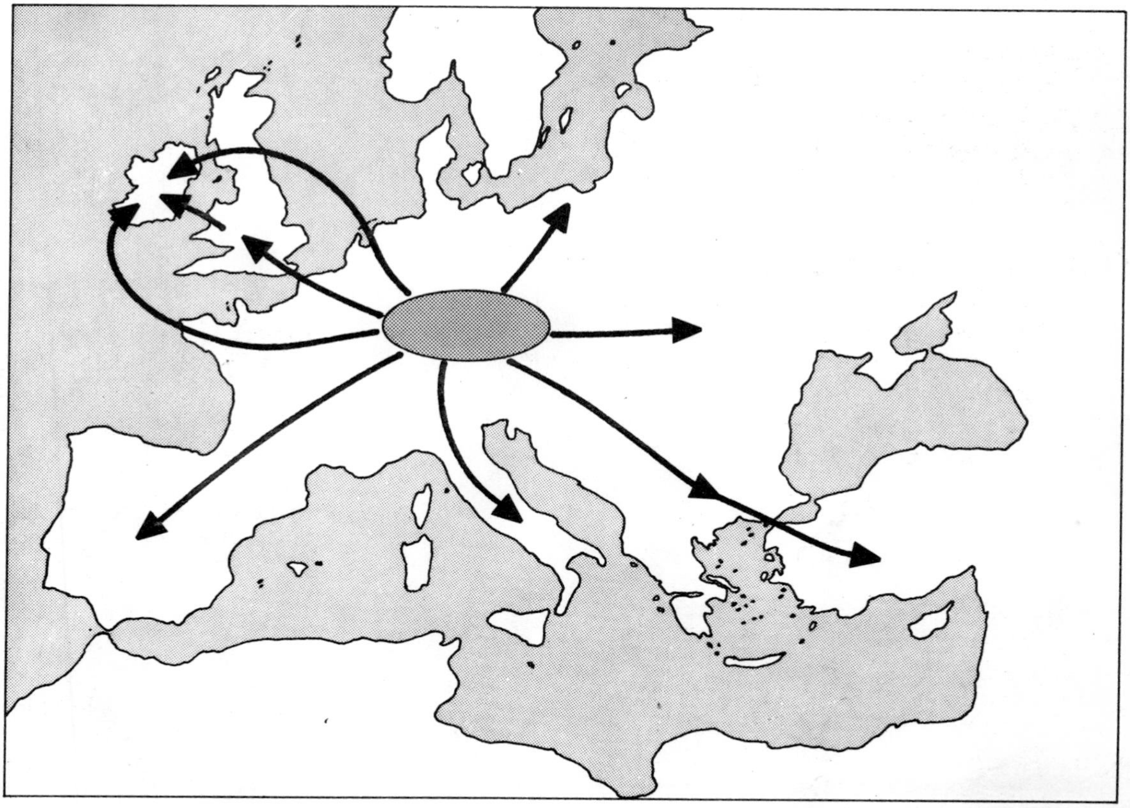

2

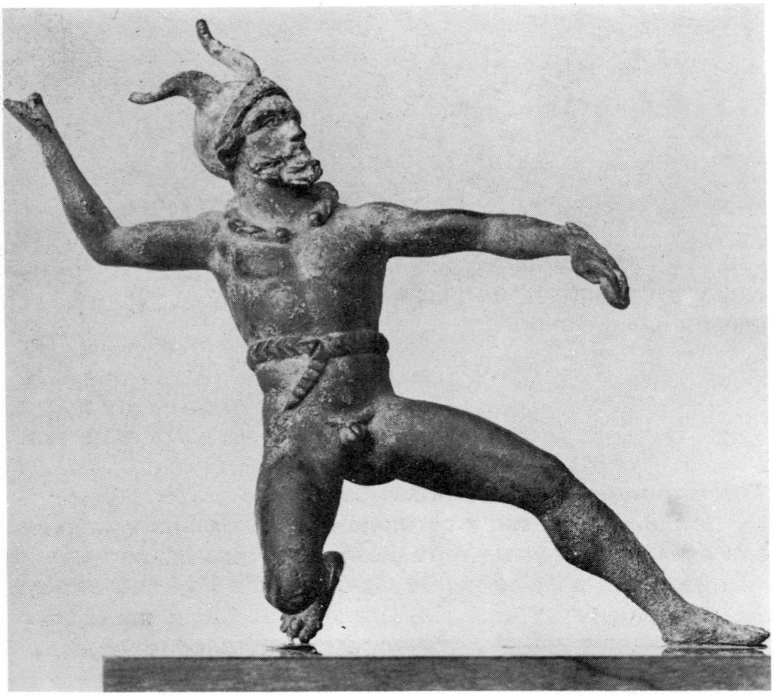

A Celtic spearman, a little bronze figure from the late third century B.C. Celtic spearmen went into battle naked and struck terror into the hearts of their opponents with their reckless bravery. Notice how this warrior is wearing a torc or Celtic neck-collar.

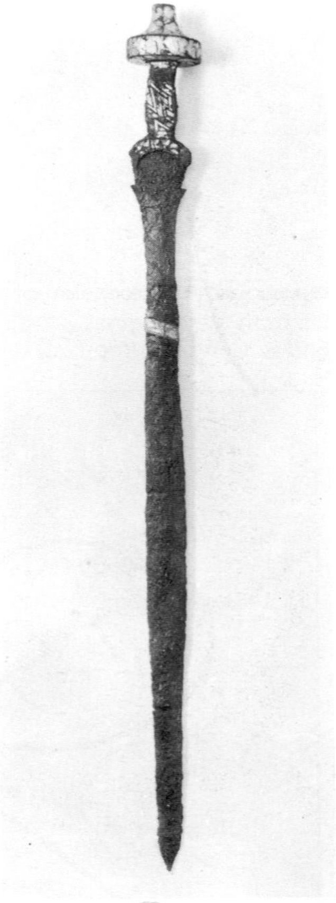

The great iron sword of the Hallstatt warriors. This sword has a gold-inlaid hilt.

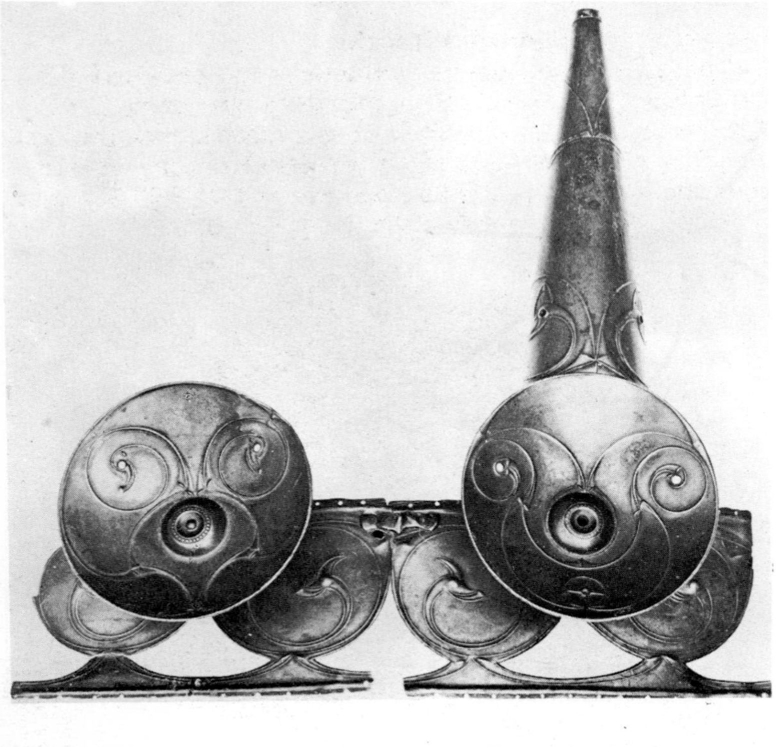

A decorated large object in metal, possibly part of a ceremonial headgear, which dates from the Iron Age.

The great stone fort at Staigue, Co. Kerry.

The gold-inlaid hilt of the Hallstatt sword.

600 B.C. there were Celts in France, Spain and Portugal. The Greek historian, Herodotus, writing about 450 B.C. says that, in his day, there were Celts along the Atlantic coast of Europe. About 400 B.C. they invaded Italy and about ten years later they sacked Rome. In 369 B.C. they were fighting as hired soldiers in Greece. In 279 B.C. a Celtic tribe sacked the shrine of Delphi in Greece and crossed over into Asia Minor where a powerful Celtic kingdom, Galatia, was set up.

From about 450 B.C. to 250 B.C. the Celts were the most powerful people in Europe. There seemed to be no end to their energy and man-power. Their kingdoms stretched from Ireland and Scotland in the north to Italy and Spain in the south, and from Asia Minor to the Atlantic coast.

The Celts in Ireland and Britain

Historians are not sure when the Celts first came to Ireland and Britain but we can be sure that there were some Celts in these islands before 600 B.C. It is probable that the first important group of Celts came to Ireland directly from the lands about the Rhine, up the North Sea and through Scotland to Ireland. We believe they came about 600 B.C.

A Celtic helmet of bronze found at Amfreville in France and preserved in the Louvre. This is a helmet in the La Tène style with enamel studs and rich decoration.

The Turoe stone, Co. Galway. This stone is ornamented in the La Tène style. Its purpose is now unknown.

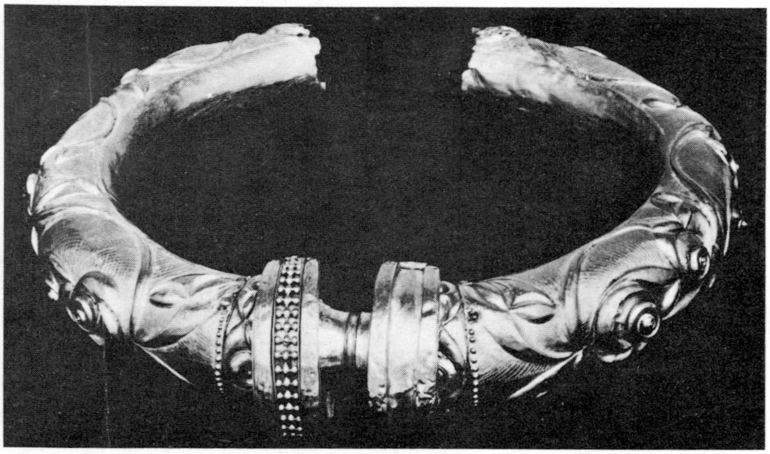

A highly decorated gold torc or neck-collar. It dates from the first century A.D. and was found at Broighter, Co. Derry.

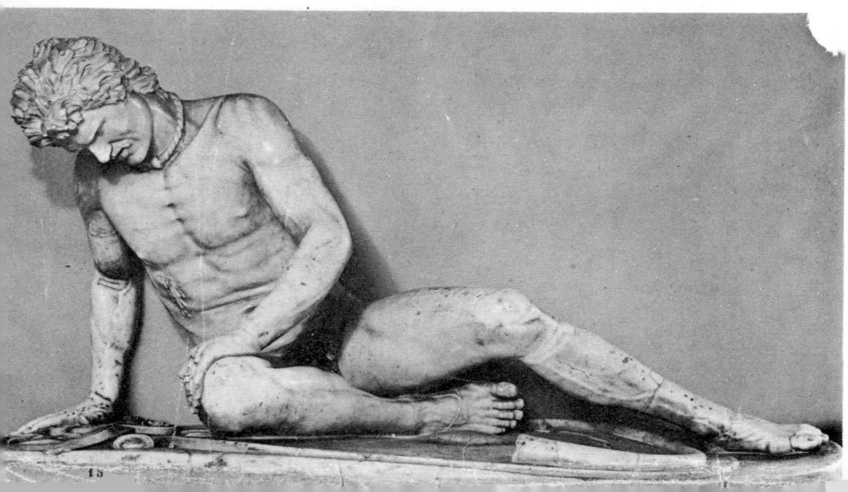

The famous 'Dying Gaul'. Notice the long hair, stiffened with lime-wash, the moustache, and the torc or neck-collar. All these are typically Celtic.

Gold ornaments from Snettisham, Norfolk. They consist of a large torc, a bracelet and a small torc. The large torc is eight inches in diameter and is beautifully ornamented. These Celtic objects were made about 50 B.C.

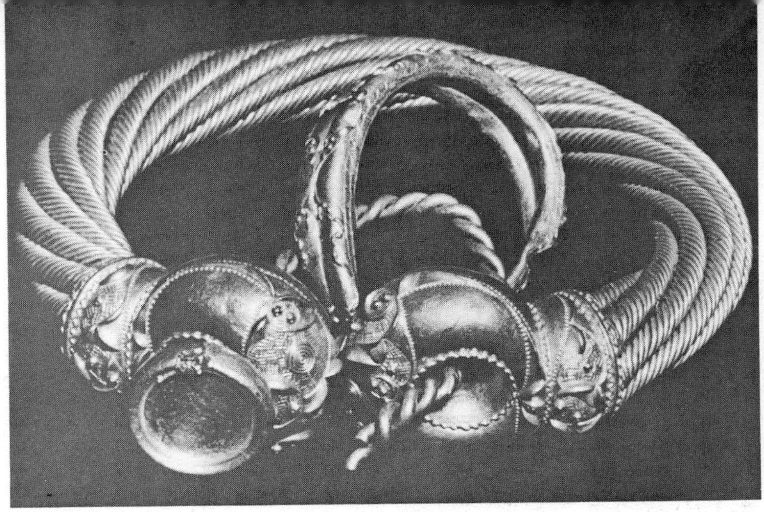

A Celtic goddess.

Hallstatt Celts: Between 500 B.C. and 400 B.C. there was a massive immigration of Celts from the Low Countries and from northern France into Britain. These were called the Hallstatt peoples from the type of weapons and ornaments they had. For 200 years they were busy expanding their conquests in Britain. They poured into the country in large numbers, over-ran the previous settlers and brought new lands under the plough. It is more than likely that some of these people crossed over to Ireland and set up some kingdoms here.

La Tène Celts: Meanwhile, some of the European Celts re-organized themselves and set out on the path of conquest again. These new groups are called La Tène Celts from the style of their weapons and ornaments. The La Tène Celts were chariot-driving warriors, like the heroes of the early Irish tales. The La Tène chiefs led the Celtic conquest of Italy and Eastern Europe. About 250 B.C. La Tène Celts from France and around the Rhine invaded Britain and between 150 and 100 B.C. they reached Ireland. This was probably the last important Celtic invasion of Ireland. Some refugees and soldiers did come from Gaul and Britain during the Roman conquest of these countries, but these cannot have been very numerous.

The Appearance and Dress of the Celts

According to ancient Greek and Roman writers, the Celts were tall and muscular with fair skin, blue eyes and blond hair. This may have been true of the nobles but in general the people were fairly mixed. Except for their long moustaches, the nobles were generally clean-shaven. The Celts wore their hair long and they used different soaps, dyes, limewashes and cosmetics generously. In dress, they were fond of bright colours. They liked striped and checked materials and from an early period they produced high-quality woollen cloth with gay patterns.

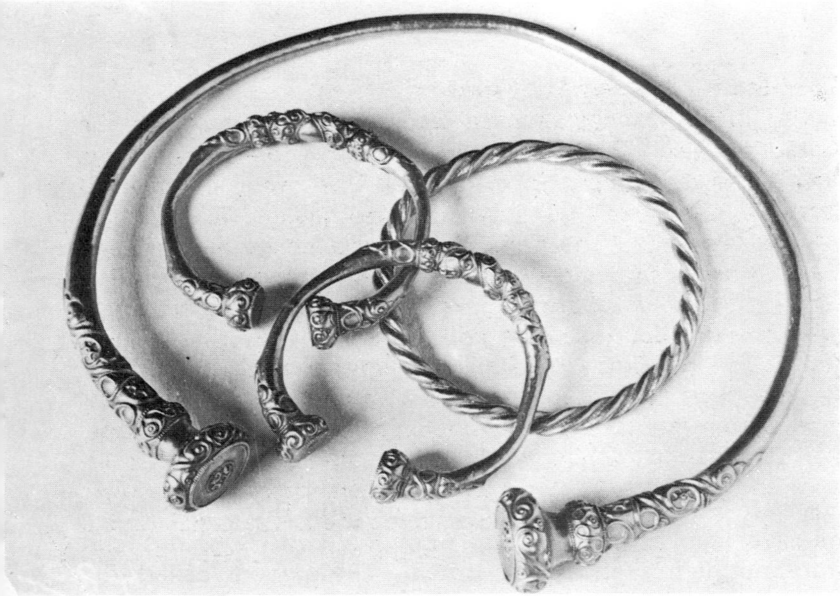

The torc, bracelets and amulets of a rich Celtic lady. These were discovered near Saarbrücken in Germany and they date from the early fourth century B.C.

The only form of writing known to the Irish was Ogham.
An Ogham stone at Kilcoolaght, near Killorglin, Co. Kerry.

In Ireland, the dress of both sexes was a *léine* or tunic of linen, worn by men to the knees and by women to the ankles. It was tied around the waist by a *criss* or belt and over this they wore a cloak of wool held in position by an ornamental brooch. They wore leather shoes or sandals of linen with leather soles. Some branches of the Celts wore trousers but trousers seem to have been the dress of the lower classes in Ireland.

Ornaments

The Celts loved gold ornaments and trinkets of bronze and silver. Their most distinctive ornament was the torc or neck-ring of gold or bronze worn by persons of high rank. Warriors wore brooches of iron, sometimes of silver. Rich women's graves show the passion for ornament: women wore finger rings, torcs, necklaces of gold, bronze and silver, bracelets, ankle-rings and splendid belts and belt-chains.

Food and Feasting

The food of the Celts consisted of beef, mutton, pork, baked salt fish and bread, but pork was the favourite dish. They imported huge quantities of wine from the Mediterranean countries and wine was drunk, particularly by the nobles. The lower classes drank beer, brewed from barley and flavoured with hops and caraway seeds. The Celts were given to feasting. The company sat down on skins, in order according to rank and prowess, and food was served on low tables. Entertainments were usual at feasts and were provided by poets and musicians.

Druids and Men of Learning

The pagan druids formed a class of their own among the Celtic peoples. They were pagan priests, foretellers of the future and men skilled in magic. But they were also men of learning, who gave legal judgments and gave advice to kings. All the learning of the druids was preserved by memory and handed down by word of mouth. After the coming of Christianity the druids gradually gave way to the Christian clergy who brought Latin learning and the art of writing as well as the Christian religion. In Christian times the *file* or poet inherited much of the authority of the druid. The duty of the *file* was to be master of the art of poetry, to praise his lord in verse, and to preserve the history of the past, the tales of the heroes, and the genealogies of the nobles. The brehons or judges were men learned in the law. They preserved the laws in ancient and difficult language and gave judgments in cases brought before them.

Religion

For the Celts of Ireland, the great religious festival was Samain, November 1, which, in their calendar, was the end of one year and the beginning of the next. Sacrifices were offered by the druids and religious rites were carried out to

An Ogham stone at Coolmagort, Co. Kerry. The writing begins at the bottom left and runs up the side of the stone.

A bronze bucket, nine inches in height, which dates from the end of the fourth century B.C. and a highly-ornamented bronze flagon (with handle and spout) which is somewhat older. These were found at Waldalgesheim and are preserved in the Landesmuseum, Bonn.

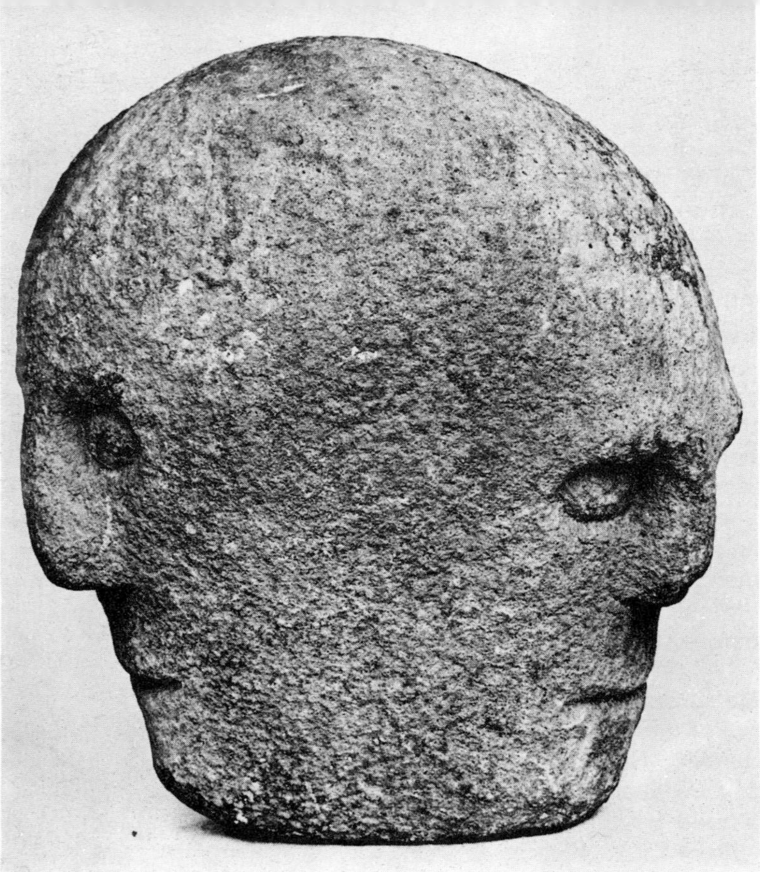

A three-faced stone head of a Celtic god, from Corleck, Co. Cavan. The Celts often thought of their gods as being trinities.

renew the fertility of the earth and its inhabitants. There were two other great festivals, Bealtaine, May 1, in honour of the old Celtic god, Belenus, and Lughnasa, August 1, in honour of the god, Lug. The chief god was An Dagda, 'the good god', who was able to do all things; he was father of the people and possessed a magic cauldron which could never be exhausted. The Celts believed in sacred trees and groves and in holy wells and rivers. They believed in an after-life, the land of the blest, to which people went after death. The Irish gods and goddesses are often called *Tuatha Dé Danann,* 'the people of the goddess Danu', and later Irish writers turned them into heroes and warriors and thought they were earlier invaders of Ireland.

The Celtic Farmers

The Celts in Ireland did not live in towns, but rather in isolated farmsteads spread throughout the country. Most of the important farmsteads were fortified with a *ráth* or earthen rampart and stood on high ground. These are what the people now call 'fairy forts'. Within the ráth lay the houses and farm buildings, and these, which were very small by modern

A stone circle at Drombeg, Co. Cork. These stone circles were used for religious purposes. They are to be found especially in Cork, Kerry and Limerick.

standards, were made of wood and covered with thatched roofs. The Celts were mixed farmers, engaged both in cultivating the soil and in cattle raising. The principal crop was barley which was used for porridge, bread-making and the brewing of beer. They also grew turnips, flax, onions, leeks, and plants to provide dyes. Later, oats became more important than barley.

However, the chief activity of Irish farmers was cattle-raising, for the grasslands of Ireland were very rich. Nobles counted their wealth in cattle, and the famous Irish epic tale, the *Táin Bó Cualgne*, is the story of a great cattle raid made into Ulster by the men of Connacht. The lands which lay around the farmsteads were cultivated and the cattle were grazed on the upland pasture and on the rough land. Herds of swine were fed on the acorns of the forest, and sheep, for which the women were responsible, were also raised.

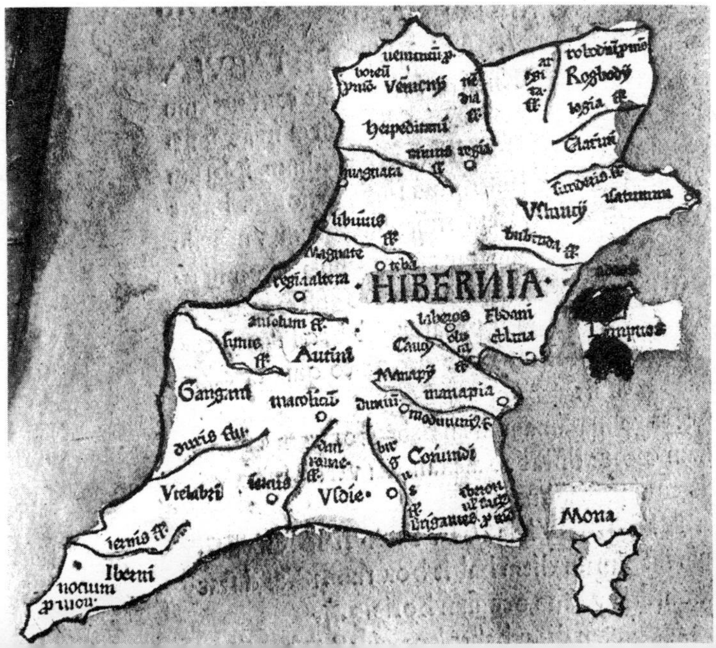

Ptolemy's map of Ireland, the earliest known map of our country. It was made about 150 A.D. Very few of the kingdoms and places marked on it can be identified with certainty.

A map of Ireland, showing the kingdoms as they were between 500 A.D. and 700 A.D.

Political Organization

Celtic Ireland was divided into about 150 tiny kingdoms called *Tuatha*, and the people within each tuath were divided into three main classes, the king, the nobles and the freemen. Each tuath had its own king, but the powers of the king were limited. He was the military leader of his people in time of war and their representative in time of peace, but he neither made the laws nor enforced them. The nobles were land-owning families and warriors. The druids, poets and some of the skilled craftsmen also belonged to this class as did the Christian clergy after the coming of Christianity. The ordinary freemen were farmers and some of the lower grades of craftsmen belonged to this class. Beneath the free classes were the unfree people, slaves and bondsmen.

A number of tuatha, joined or allied together, made up a local kingdom which was ruled by a greater king. The kingdom of Ossory, which was about as large as the present diocese of Ossory, was such a local kingdom. A group of local kingdoms joined together made up an overkingdom or provincial kingdom. There was no high-king or King of all Ireland and the highest grade of king known to the Irish was the king of a province.

The Kingdoms of Ireland

In the fifth and sixth centuries Ireland was divided into a number of powerful overkingdoms. Over Northern Ireland stretched the great kingdom of the *Ulaid*, who ruled over many smaller kingdoms and subject races. In the west were the *Connachta*, who gave their name to the province of Connacht. A branch of the Connachta, called Uí Néill from their great ancestor Niall of the Nine Hostages, conquered a great portion of northern Ireland, drove the Ulaid eastwards and set up kingdoms there. These are called the Northern Uí Néill. They also conquered the midlands and set up kingdoms in Westmeath and Meath. These are called the Southern Uí Néill. In time the Uí Néill became the most powerful kings in Ireland and they later claimed to be high-kings or kings of all Ireland. In Munster the most important kings were the kings of *Eoghanachta*, who ruled a string of kingdoms stretching from Cashel to Loch Léin and claimed to be kings of all Munster. In the south east of Ireland, stretching from the Liffey to the sea at Wexford, were the kings of *Laigin*, who gave their name to Leinster. They were a warlike people who defended themselves for centuries against the attacks of the Uí Néill.

Beneath these great kingdoms were the small kingdoms ruled by the less powerful families like the Corca Loígde, Déise,

Lóigis, Airgialla etc. These had once been powerful but were now conquered. Many of them had to pay tribute to the greater kings and support them in battle.

Things to Do

1. Imagine that you were a king in early Ireland. Write an account of your day's activities—what you would wear, eat, drink, how you would amuse yourself and what people you would be likely to meet.
2. Caesar's *De Bello Gallico*, which you read in your Latin class, is Caesar's own account of how he conquered the Gauls, a Celtic people. See what information about the Celts can you gather from Caesar's account.
3. In the National Museum there are many objects which belonged to the Celts and to the people who went before them. Arrange a visit to the museum and see these objects.

Books to Read or Consult

Joseph Raftery (ed.) *The Celts*, Cork 1964. This book contains a great deal of information about the languages, history and customs of the Celts.

K. H. Jackson, *The Oldest Irish Tradition*, Cambridge 1964.

T. G. E. Powell, *The Celts*, London 1958.

M. Dillon and N. Chadwick, *The Celtic Realms*, London 1967 is full of information about the Celts. These books may be a little difficult for you. Your teacher will help you and, anyway, you will enjoy the beautiful photographs of Celtic ornaments and objects.

Ireland and the Coming of Christianity

Ireland and Rome

Ireland never formed part of the Roman Empire as did Britain and many of the old Celtic lands. As a result, the native kingdoms and the native culture survived and kept their independence in Ireland. However, Ireland was not isolated and cut off from the rest of Europe. The Roman writer, Tacitus, has mention of the busy trade that went on between Ireland and the Roman Empire. Ireland exported hides, cattle and the famous Irish wolfhounds. She imported wine, oil, pottery, glass and other articles. But when the power of the Roman Empire began to decline in the fourth and fifth centuries, the Irish traders turned into raiders who plundered Roman Britain for gold and valuables and for slaves. According to tradition, Niall of the Nine Hostages was one of the great leaders of such raids.

Irish Colonies in Britain

Eventually, the Irish raiders conquered and settled in parts of Britain, and they set up kingdoms all along the west coast of Britain. In Wales, the Laigin, the Déisi, and the Uí Liatháin set up and ruled kingdoms in the fourth and fifth centuries. In the north, the people of the Irish kingdom of Dál Riada conquered the western isles of Scotland and eventually founded a powerful Gaelic kingdom in Scotland. The Irish kingdoms in Wales and in the south did not survive, but the Irish kingdom of Dál Riada eventually became the kingdom of Scotland.

The First Irish Christians

Christianity spread slowly westwards along the Mediterranean. At first Christians were persecuted by the Romans, but in 313 Constantine the Great (274–337) issued the famous Edict of Milan which gave the Church official recognition and encouragement. The Celtic lands slowly became Christian. Parts of Gaul were Christian by the second century, but by 395 the whole country was organized into dioceses with bishops ruling and living in the towns. We know that by the year 200 there were Christians in parts of Britain under Roman rule. By 350 the Church in Britain was well organized and had its own bishops.

We do not know when Christianity first reached Ireland, but it is certain that by the year 400 there were some Christian communities here. Some very early traditions have it that the

habent unum Christum per illum illamque
intuitus multas per[illegible]
Uin est rex christianus uindumi ait
O mea Brittania parrochia tua in
prouincia tua apud [illegible] mo
narchiam quam imperante Romanorum
[illegible] et occidentali dominatu [illegible]

Incipiunt libri sancti Patricii episcopi

Ego Patricius peccator rusticissimus et minimus omnium fidelium et contemptibilis sum apud plurimos.

Patrem habui Calpornum diaconum filium quendam Potiti prespiteri (filii Odissi) qui fuit uico bannauem taberniae. Uillulam enim prope habuit ubi ego capturam dedi. Annorum eram tunc fere xui. Deum enim uerum ignorabam et Hibernione in captiuitate adductus sum cum tot milia hominum secundum merita nostra quia a deo recessimus et praecepta eius non custodiuimus et sacerdotibus nostris non oboedientes fuimus qui nostram salutem admonebant et dominus induxit super nos iram animationis suae et dispersit nos in gentibus multis etiam usque ad ultimum terrae ubi nunc paruitas mea esse uidetur inter alienigenas et ibi dominus aperuit sensum incredulitatis meae ut uel sero rememorarem delicta mea et ut conuerterem toto corde ad dominum deum meum qui respexit humilitatem meam et misertus est adoliscentiae et ignorantiae meae et custodiuit me antequam scirem eum et antequam saperem uel distinguerem inter bonum et malum et muniuit me et consulatus est me ut pater filium.

Unde autem tacere non possum neque expedit quidem tanta beneficia et tantam gratiam quam mihi dignatus est in terra captiuitatis meae quia haec est retributio nostra ut post correptionem uel agnitionem dei exaltare et confiteri mirabilia eius coram omni natione quae est sub omni caelo quia non est alius deus nec umquam fuit nec ante nec erit post haec praeter deum patrem ingenitum sine principio a quo est omne principium omnia tenentem ut didicimus et huius filium Iesum Christum qui cum patre scilicet semper fuisse testamur ante originem saeculi spiritaliter apud patrem inenarrabiliter genitum ante omne principium et per ipsum facta sunt uisibilia hominem factum morte deuicta in caelis ad patrem receptum et dedit illi omnem potestatem super omne nomen caelestium et terrestrium et infernorum et omnis lingua confiteatur ei quia dominus et deus est Iesus Christus quem credimus et expectamus aduentum ipsius mox futurum iudex uiuorum atque mortuorum qui reddet unicuique secundum facta sua et effudit in uobis habunde spiritum sanctum donum et pignus inmortalitatis qui facit credentes et oboedientes ut sint filii dei et coheredes Christi quem confitemur et adoramus unum deum in trinitate sacri nominis. Ipse enim dixit per profetam: Inuoca me in die tribulationis tuae et liberabo te et magnificabis me.

The beginning of St Patrick's *Confession* from the Book of Armagh.

south of Ireland, the part of Ireland most in contact with Gaul, was first to receive Christianity. It may have been brought by wine merchants and other traders, by Irish contacts with Britain and perhaps by scholars from Roman Gaul, fleeing before the barbarian invasions. By 431 the Christian communities in Ireland had grown large enough to require a bishop and in that year Pope Celestine ordained Palladius and sent him as first bishop to the Irish believing in Christ. We know very little about the mission of Palladius but it seems that he and other missionaries laboured in the east and south of Ireland with some success.

St Patrick the Briton

However, it is the British missionary, Patrick, who received the credit for the conversion of Ireland. He became the Christian hero of Ireland. Because of his popularity, because he left writings behind him, and because of the writings of the clergy of Armagh, a great number of stories and legends grew up about St Patrick from the seventh century on, and it is now very difficult to separate fact from fiction. We do not know when exactly he came to Ireland, how long his mission was, or when he died. However, it is likely that he was working in this country from about 460 to 490.

St Patrick left behind him two documents, *The Letter to Coroticus*, and a work written in his old age, *The Confessions*. These two documents contain all that we know with certainty about St Patrick. He tells us that his father was a well-off official in a city in Roman Britain. The family had an estate and villa near the city and Patrick was captured on the estate by Irish raiders and sold into slavery in Ireland. At this time he was about sixteen years of age. For six years he tended sheep for his Irish master. In his loneliness he turned to God in prayer and he tells us he prayed a hundred times in a single day and almost as many times in the night. At last he heard a voice which said: 'Look, your ship is ready'. He made his escape and travelled about 200 miles to the coast, boarded a ship manned by pagan Irish sailors and, after many adventures, made his way back to his own people in Britain. However, he had visions and he heard the voices of the Irish asking him to return to them. Patrick took this as a command from God to go as a missionary to the Irish. He does not tell us where he received his clerical training, but it is likely that he received some of it in Gaul. He was ordained, and, despite the objections of his superiors who thought him unsuitable, he set out with his companions on his great mission to the Irish. He seems to have been most active in the midlands, the west and the north. He was

A medieval statue of St Patrick in St Patrick's Cathedral, Dublin. This statue captures the strength of Patrick's character and his loneliness as a missionary among strangers.

constantly on the move, accompanied by a retinue of nobles, preaching, baptizing and founding churches. He made thousands of converts, ordained priests everywhere and organized the Irish Church. Patrick, as we know from his writings, was a humble man who made no claim to learning or holiness. He says of himself: 'I am Patrick, a sinner, most unlearned, the least of all the faithful and utterly despised by many'. His enemies believed him unsuitable for his mission but Patrick insisted that, unworthy as he was, he had received a divine call to convert the Irish. Patrick then was the greatest of the missionaries to the Irish and well deserves the name of national apostle.

The Early Irish Church

Ireland was not converted to Christianity in a single generation. For a long time the learned orders, the judges and poets, stood out against the new religion. For a hundred years after the coming of St Patrick large areas of the country and a large part of the population were pagan, or Christian in name only. We even have Irish Church laws from the sixth century laying

An air-photograph of Tara of the kings. From here the great prehistoric kings of our legends ruled and here Diarmait Mac Cearbaill celebrated the pagan feast of Tara in 560.

down how the Christian is to behave towards his pagan neighbours. The most important kings, the Uí Néill kings, seem to have remained pagan for several generations. As late as 560, King Diarmait Mac Cearbaill still celebrated the pagan feast of Tara and he was cursed by the clergy for doing so. Indeed, Diarmait, who died in 560, may have been the last of the great pagan kings. And even when the country became officially Christian, many pagan beliefs and practices survived in spite of Christianity.

The Church set up in this country by St Patrick and the other missionaries was an episcopal Church. The country was divided up into dioceses, each ruled by a bishop. The diocese corresponded in boundary to the Irish petty kingdoms and each diocese had a number of churches which the bishop visited from time to time. In the beginning, most priests and bishops were married; later clerics were unmarried. The clergy shaved their heads and wore tunics to distinguish themselves from the pagans.

Things to Do

1. St Patrick's *Confession* written in Latin, has been translated into English and Irish. Get a copy of it, read it and write a short account of him; what sort of person was he?
2. Why is St Patrick called the national apostle of Ireland?

Books to Read or Consult

M. & L. de Paor, *Early Christian Ireland,* London 1958.
Eoin Mac Neill, *St Patrick*, Dublin 1964.
John Ryan (ed.), *St Patrick*, Dublin 1958.

Monks and Scholars

The chief monasteries of early Christian Ireland. Notice the large number of monasteries in the midland belt.

The ruins of the early monastery of Sceilg, Co. Kerry. The monastery is on a lonely and barren island, eight miles from the mainland.

The Monastic Movement

In the course of his mission St Patrick encouraged Irishmen and women to become monks and virgins of Christ, but we do not know if any monasteries were founded at this time. However, monasticism was growing very popular in the western Church and by 500 there were some very important monasteries in Britain. The Irish Church was always in close contact with Britain and many Irishmen studied in British monasteries. St Énna returned from Britain and about 490 he founded a famous monastery in the Aran Islands where many Irishmen learned the monastic way of life. St Finian, under the influence of the British saints, Cadoc and Gildas, founded Clonard about 510.

The founding of Clonmacnoise (540 or 550 A.D.) from a detail on the Cross of the Scriptures, Clonmacnoise.

Gallarus Oratory, Co. Kerry, a beautiful and sturdily built stone church. Local people believe that if they can squeeze themselves through the narrow window of the oratory they will surely go to Heaven.

The monks of Clonard were famous not only for their holiness but also for their learning and St Finian is called 'the teacher of the saints in Ireland'. St Ciarán founded Clonmacnoise about 540 or 550. After 550 came many more foundations. St Brendan founded Clonfert, St Comgall founded Bangor, and the greatest of the Irish saints, St Columcille founded Derry and Durrow. About 563 he crossed over to the western isles of Scotland and founded Iona. There were also foundations for women, the most famous being that of St Brighid at Kildare. A great number of monasteries were founded in deserted and barren places, away from the affairs of men, and here the monks, like those of Sceilg or Glendalough, sought solitude and holiness.

The Irish made use of their knowledge of the scriptures in their stonework. Here is the temptation of Adam and Eve by the Serpent, from the High Cross at Moone, Co. Kildare.

The ruins of Clonmacnoise, one of the greatest centres of Irish holiness and learning. Here were written the Book of the Dun Cow, some books of annals and many famous manuscripts.

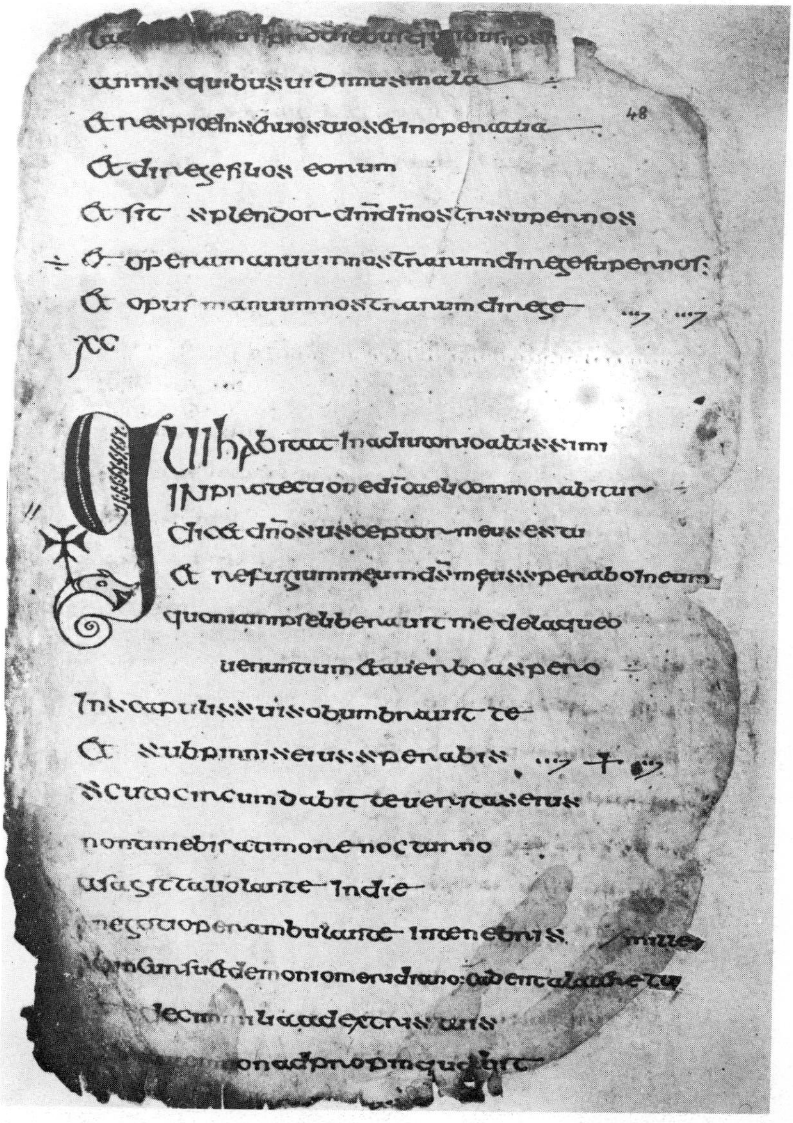

annis quibus uidimus mala
Et respice in seruos tuos et in opera tua 48
Et dirige filios eorum
Et sit splendor dñi dei nostri super nos
Et opera manuum nostrarum dirige super nos
Et opus manuum nostrarum dirige
XC
Qui habitat in adiutorio altissimi
in protectione dei caeli commorabitur
Dicet dño susceptor meus es tu
Et refugium meum dš meus sperabo in eum
quoniam ipse liberauit me de laqueo
uenantium et a uerbo aspero
In scapulis suis obumbrauit te
Et sub pinnis eius sperabis
Scuto circumdabit te ueritas eius
non timebis a timore nocturno
a sagitta uolante in die
a negotio perambulante in tenebris

A page from the *Cathach*, a manuscript of the Psalms, supposed to have been written by Columcille himself.

A scribe in the scriptorium, from the Book of Kells.

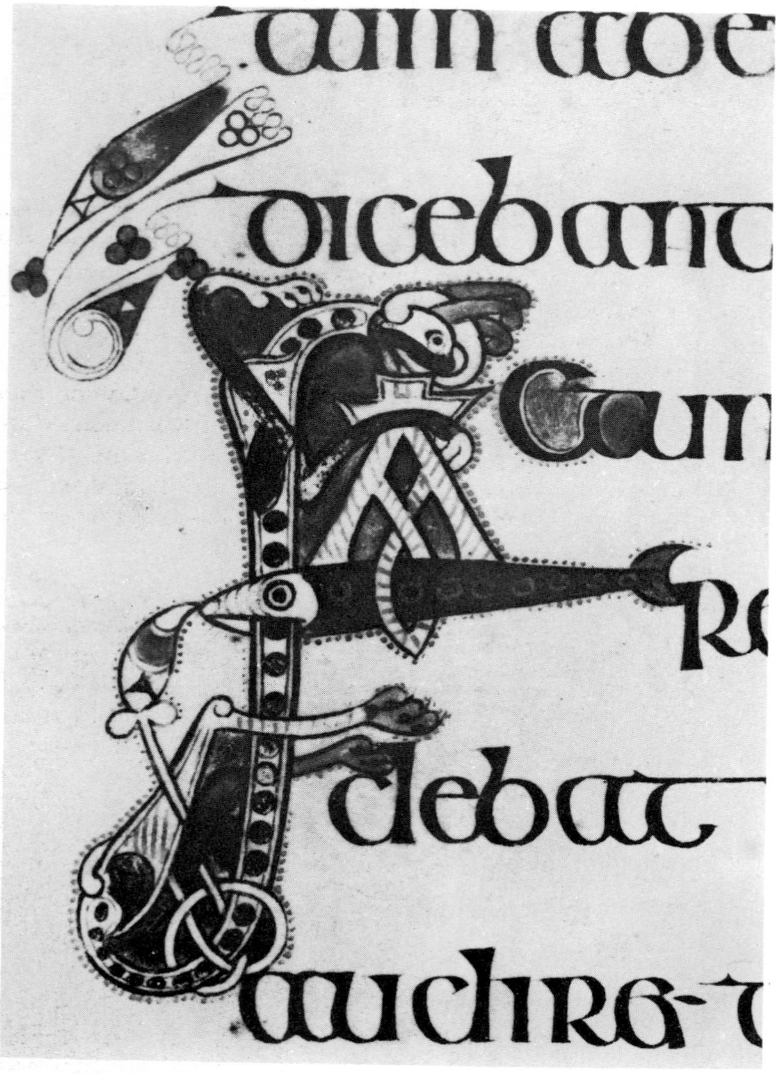

Ornamented capital from the Book of Kells, showing its typical and complicated designs.

The Book of Kells, one of the world's finest illuminated manuscripts.

Abbots and Bishops

From about 550 forward, the abbots and their monasteries became more important than the bishops in their dioceses. The Irish took up the monastic ideal with enthusiasm. Lands were granted to the monasteries and they increased in number and in power. Many monasteries founded daughter-houses throughout Ireland and in Britain and continental Europe. The head or abbot of a group of monasteries became more important than any bishop and eventually the bishops themselves adopted the monastic way of life. In Ireland from about 600 the Church was ruled by abbots; in Christian Europe the Church was ruled by bishops and this was the main difference between the Church in Ireland and the Church in Europe.

Drawings of a fish and a cat from the Book of Kells.

The eagle, the symbol of St John the evangelist from the Book of Kells.

Life in an Irish Monastery

The monastic buildings were surrounded by a ráth, a circular bank with a ditch outside it. Within this enclosure stood the main buildings of the monastery, the church, the refectory, the guest-house, the cells of the monks and the schools. The church was made of hewn oak planks and roofed with thatch of reed or rushes. Most of the rest of the buildings were made of wattle and daub. In the islands off the west coast, where timber was scarce, the monastic buildings were made of stone, and this gradually became the custom in the rest of Ireland. There are still several hundred tiny stone churches, dating from the eighth and ninth centuries, to be seen throughout Ireland. By modern standards, the monastic buildings, and even the churches, were tiny. Most of the early churches are no more than fifteen feet by ten. Even when the monastery grew in size, the monks preferred to build several small churches rather than one large one.

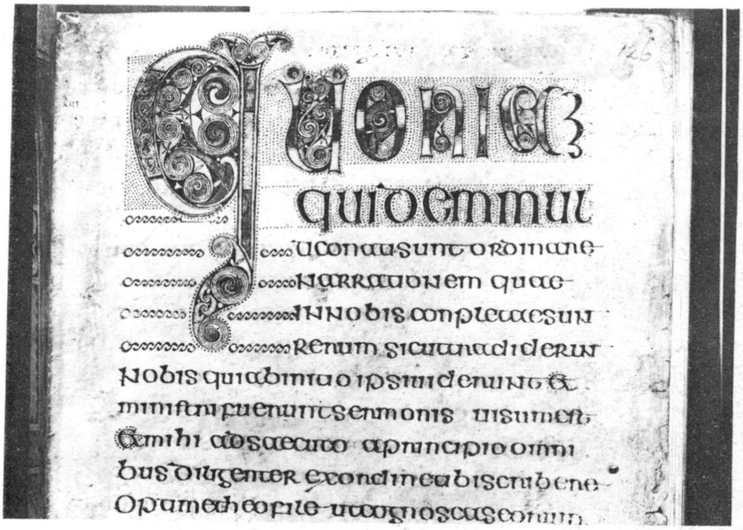

A page from the Book of Durrow.

The beginning of the gospel of St John from the Book of Dimma.

The Work of the Monks

The Irish monastery was completely self-supporting. The monks lived under a strict monastic rule and divided their day between prayer, manual labour and study. They lived a life of strict chastity and obedience and did severe penance for even the tiniest fault. Sundays, the great feasts of the Church, and the feast-days of the saints were celebrated with full church ceremony. Wednesdays and Fridays were days of severe fast and no food was taken until late evening. The monks assembled daily at the canonical hours and chanted the office. Their manual work was chiefly farming and the abbot himself was not above working the farm. The monks ploughed, sowed and reaped the harvest. Other monks produced the various tools and equipment required in the monastery. Near the monastic buildings were the forge and workshops, the barns, the mill and the lime kiln. In monasteries beside the sea or rivers, the monks spent a great deal of their time fishing. When they sat around the long table in the refectory the food they ate was all the produce of their own labours—bread, milk, fish and eggs. Meat was allowed on feastdays and on the arrival of guests. The dress of the monks was a tunic or under-garment, a heavy cape or mantle and a cowl. When working or travelling they wore leather sandals. At night they retired to their little cells and slept in their habits on straw mattresses covered with skins.

Learning in the Irish Monasteries

The monasteries were not only centres of piety; they were also important centres of learning and study. The novices were taught how to read and write Latin. They took notes and wrote their compositions on waxen tablets with a metal stylus or pen. The principal textbook of the students was the Bible, and especially the Psalms, which they learned by heart. Latin grammar was very closely studied and the monks may have known a little Greek. They were expected to know the Old and New Testament and the commentaries of the Fathers of the Church. They also read the lives of the Saints and the works of the Christian authors. It is believed that the ancient pagan authors, Virgil, Horace, Ovid and others were read and studied in Irish monasteries. Scholars flocked from England to study in the famous Irish schools, and the English historian, Bede, says that they were received kindly by the Irish, given board and lodgings for nothing, and a free education.

The Copying of Manuscripts

The copying of manuscripts, and particularly of gospel books, was an important duty for the monks. Naturally only a few

Precious manuscripts were kept in a protective box or shrine. This is the shrine of the Book of Armagh.

of the monks could be trained in the difficult art of copying and illuminating. The copyists worked in the scriptorium or writing-room of the monastery. In the scriptorium was an adequate supply of quills and ink. The monks wrote on vellum, the skins of calves which were cured, pared, rubbed and made suitable for writing on. The books were preserved in leather satchels and hung on the walls of the scriptorium. One of our earliest manuscripts is the *Cathach*, a copy of Psalms supposed to have been made by Columcille himself. This early manuscript has some ornamentation, but as time went on the decoration and illumination of manuscripts became more elaborate and more beautiful. The monasteries founded by St Columcille carried on a wonderful tradition of copying which eventually produced such masterpieces as the *Book of Durrow* and the *Book of Kells*. These manuscripts were decorated

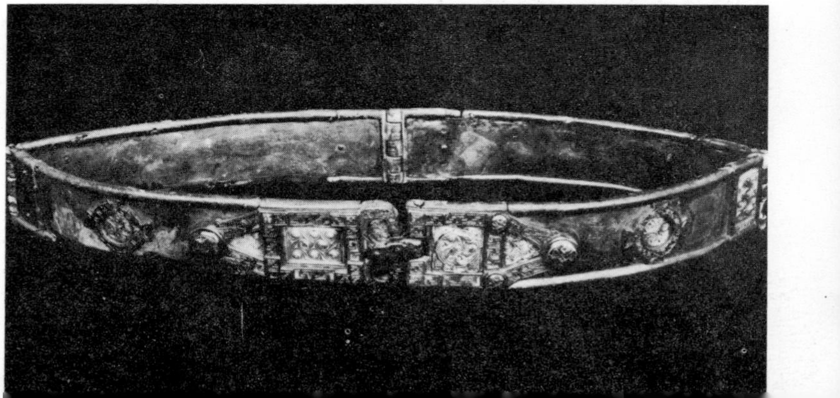

The Moylough Belt Shrine. It is made of tinned bronze, ornamented with enamel and silver panels. It was made about 750 A.D. to enshrine the leather belt of a saint.

with wonderful spirals, scrolls and patterns in dark-brown, yellow, green and vermilion. Indeed the Book of Kells is regarded as one of the world's finest illuminated manuscripts. During his visit to Ireland, Gerald the Welshman saw an Irish illuminated manuscript and he was so impressed that he declared that 'it must have been the result of the work, not of men, but of angels'. One monk tells us how much he enjoys copying in the woods:

Woodland hedges shadow me
The blackbird's song sings to me
Over my many-lined book
The birds' trill rings to me.
The clear cuckoo calls to me
In his grey cloak from the coppice.
Truly God is good to me.
I write well in the forest.

The centre-piece of the Tara brooch showing the delicate and intricate metalwork.

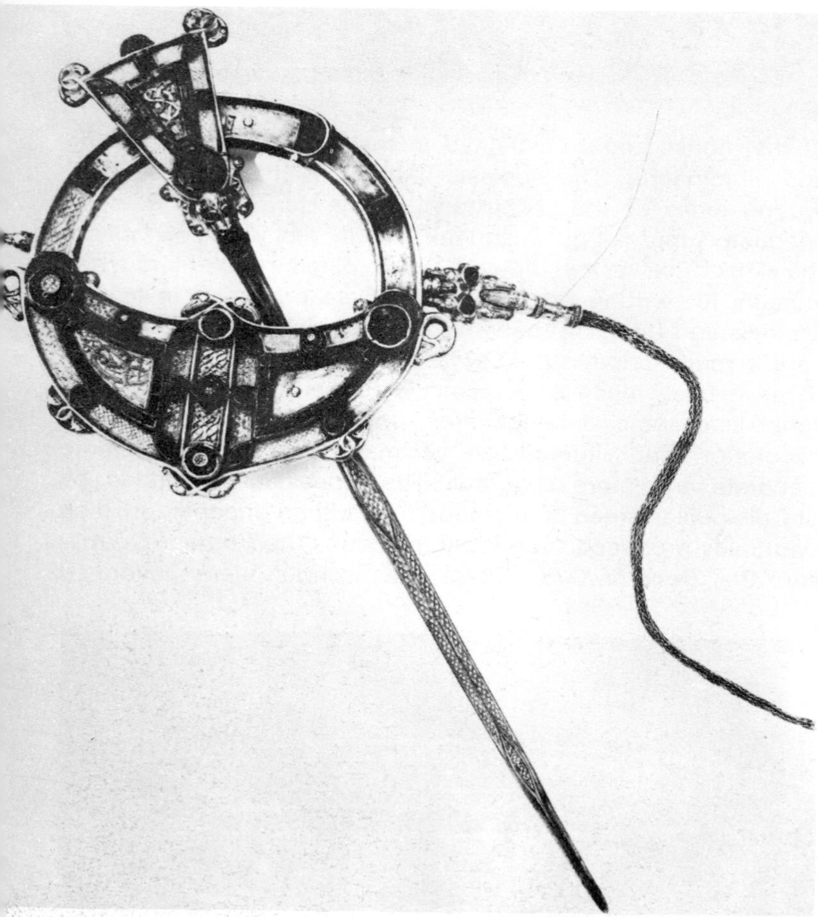

The Tara brooch, one of the greatest treasures of Irish metalwork. It dates from about 700 A.D. and was discovered on the seashore, near Drogheda.

The Ardagh chalice, a large silver chalice, decorated with gold. It dates from about 750 A.D. and it was found at Ardagh, Co. Limerick.

Metal-Work and Sculpture

With the gradual growth in the power and wealth of the monasteries the Church became the great patron of the metal workers. The relics of the saints and the precious books of the monasteries were enclosed in reliquaries and shrines of the finest metal work. The tradition of Irish metal working goes back to prehistoric times, but the Irish metal workers now learned new patterns and methods, especially from the Anglo-Saxons. Two of the finest products of Irish metal workers are the Tara

The handle of the Ardagh Chalice. Notice the delicate workmanship and the intricate spirals.

brooch and the Ardagh chalice. The Tara brooch is made of cast bronze, beautifully and delicately ornamented with interlacing animal patterns. The Ardagh chalice is a heavy silver chalice decorated with gold, glass, and enamel and ornamented with delicate and elaborate patterns.

The Bell of Armagh, a cast bronze bell with an inscription asking a prayer for Cumascach, son of Ailill, who died in 904.

An early Christian memorial slab at Clonmacnoise with an inscription in Irish asking a prayer for Mael-Finnia. From these slabs developed the beautiful sculptured stone crosses of a later period.

Eight of the twelve apostles from the great granite high-cross at Moone, Co. Kildare.

The Irish artists brought over to stone-carving and sculpture many of the patterns they used so successfully in book ornamentation and metal-work. The famous Irish high crosses developed from the crosses used in processions and set up on monastic sites. The cross itself was ringed and the surface of it was covered with fine carvings and decorative stone-work.

Daniel in the lions' den, from the high cross at Moone.

The Monks and Native Learning

Side by side with the monastic schools were the schools of the native Irish poets and judges, which had a history stretching back to ancient times. The judges preserved the ancient laws of the Irish in difficult and obscure verses and taught the laws to their students in the law schools. The poets were not only poets but also men of learning. They wrote praise-poems in honour of the kings and nobles. They preserved the early history of the Irish and the genealogies of the ruling families. They also preserved the ancient literature and tales, and the poet was bound to know 150 tales by heart. The poets received an intense training and they spent seven years at school before they were recognized as poets and men of learning. All the knowledge of the poets was preserved by memory and handed down in the schools by word of mouth from generation to generation. But by the seventh century the poets and judges had become Christian; they learned the art of writing from the monks and they wrote down their traditional knowledge. The monks knew and loved the old tales of the warriors and kings and they copied them into their manuscripts and preserved them for future generations. But it is likely that lay scribes were also active in the seventh and eighth centuries, in writing down the ancient laws and the tales of the pagan gods and heroes. In Ireland, then, there was a remarkable mixture of Irish and Latin learning, and due to this Ireland has the most interesting and valuable early literature of all the European countries.

Things to Do

1. Ask your teacher to get you a map of monastic Ireland. Find out what monasteries were situated in your locality and discover as much as you can about them.
2. Who are the patron saints of your diocese and of your locality? What is known of their lives and miracles; are there any holy wells dedicated to them? When you have found out as much as you can, write an account of them.
3. Ask the librarian to let you see a copy of L. Bieler, *Ireland, Harbinger of the Middle Ages*. In this book you will see beautiful photographs of the manuscripts and churches of the early Irish monks.

Books to Read or Consult

M. & L. de Paor, *Early Christian Ireland*, London 1958.
Alice Curtayne, *More Tales of Irish Saints*, Dublin 1957.
D. C. Pochin Mould, *The Irish Saints*, Dublin 1964.
G. O. Simms, *The Book of Kells*, Dublin 1961.
Françoise Henry, *Early Christian Irish Art*, Dublin 1955.

Missionaries and Teachers

As soon as the Christian faith had taken firm root in this country, Irish monks set out as missionaries and 'pilgrims for Christ'. Europe had been devastated by the invasions of the barbarians who poured over the borders in the fifth century, and in many parts of the Continent Christian life and learning had reached a low ebb. Christian Britain had been conquered by the pagan Angles and Saxons who made the greater part of England pagan again. In Scotland the Picts were for the most part pagans.

Many of the Irish missionaries did not go abroad in the first place as missionaries, but as 'pilgrims for Christ'. They went into exile as a penance. Exile was one of the greatest punishments in Irish law and an Irish monk compared it to martyrdom when he wrote: 'It is white martyrdom when a man parts with everything he loves for the sake of God'. But the Irish monks soon took up the work of preaching the Gospel, founding monasteries and reviving Christian learning. So great was their success that one German scholar has said that the Irish 'shaped decisively the religious and cultural life of England and of Western and Central Europe for several centuries'.

St Columcille

St Columcille belonged by birth to the first nobility of Ireland, to the Northern Uí Néill. Three of his first cousins were Uí Néill kings, and he himself could have been a king but he chose to be a monk. He founded a famous monastery at Durrow, and in 546 he founded another at Derry. But Columcille wished to be an exile for Christ, and in 563 he crossed over, with twelve companions, to the western isles of Scotland and

The idea of exile—'pilgrimage for Christ'—was very much present to the Irish monks. Here is a carving of Christ's own exile—the flight into Egypt—from the high cross at Moone, Co. Kildare.

The small stone oratory, known as Columcille's house, at Kells, Co. Meath, built in 814 by monks fleeing from Iona because of the Viking attacks.

founded his monastery on the little island of Iona. To the south-east of Iona was the kingdom of Dál Riada (founded by the Irish) and in the Highlands lay the kingdoms of pagan Picts. Columcille's greatest achievements was the conversion of the Picts. For about thirty-two years he laboured in Scotland, and he is recognized as the founder of the Christian Church in Scotland. But Columcille did not cut himself off from Ireland. He was present at the Convention of Druim Cetta (574 or 578) where he settled the quarrel between the Irish at home and the Irish in Scotland. He governed his monasteries in Ireland by messengers from Iona and he kept in close touch with affairs in Ireland. Tradition says he was the protector of the poets, and that he himself was a poet. He died about 597 and was buried in Iona.

The Continuation of Columcille's Mission

Columcille's successors in Iona continued his missionary effort. The most northern kingdom of the Anglo-Saxons was Northumbria. At one time Oswald, king of Northumbria, was a refugee at Iona and became a Christian. When he became king in 635 he invited Irish monks from Iona to preach the

A new statue of St Columbanus erected at Luxeuil, the site of his great monastery. It was unveiled in 1950 in the presence of Pope John XXIII (then papal nuncio to France) and President de Valera.

An illuminated page from the St Chad gospels, Lichfield Cathedral.

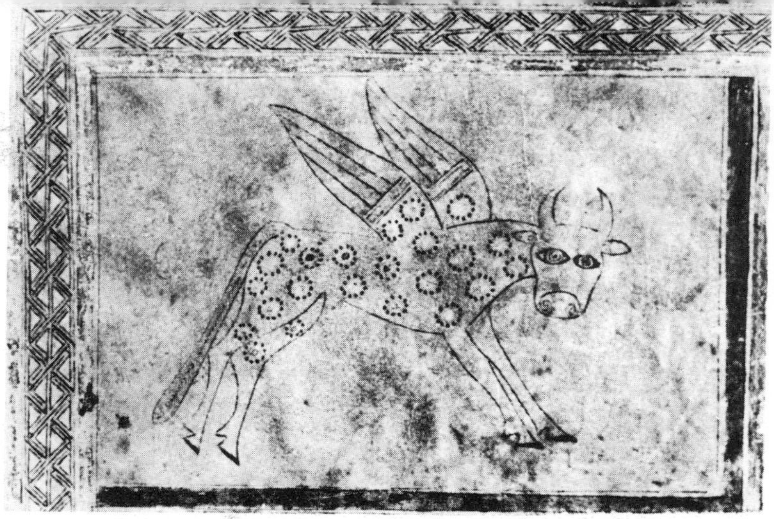

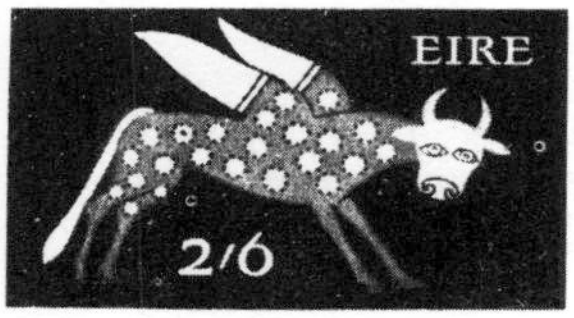

The design of this Irish stamp is based on the figure in the St Chad gospels.

The tomb of St Columbanus in the crypt of the St Columban Church in Bobbio, Northern Italy. The church was formerly attached to the abbey of Bobbio, where Columbanus died in 615.

The library of the former monastery of St Gall, Switzerland. Many of the earliest surviving manuscripts from Irish monasteries are preserved here, including some of the oldest specimens of written Irish.

Gospel in his kingdom. The greatest of the missionaries to Northumbria was St Aidán who founded his monastic church in Lindisfarne. He and his successors, St Finán and St Colmán, completed the conversion of Northumbria and began missions to the other Anglo-Saxon kingdoms.

The Anglo-Saxons of the south had already received Christianity, for Pope Gregory the Great had sent the monk Augustine as a missionary to them in 597. The Papal mission worked its way northwards and the Irish monks moved gradually southwards to meet them. The Irish differed in a number of things from the Papal mission; they celebrated Easter according to the old reckoning and they had their own special tonsure. Bitter disputes followed and these came to a head at the Synod of Whitby (664) where Roman customs won the day. St Colmán, the leader of the Irish party withdrew with his monks, but the influence of Irish monks and teachers continued for a long time in England. The Church in Northumbria kept in close touch with Ireland, and the Irish style of manuscript writing continued there.

St Columbanus (c.540–615)

Columbanus was a Leinsterman of noble family and good education. He decided to become a monk and he studied and lived under the severe rule of St Comgall at Bangor. At the age of fifty he set out from Bangor with twelve companions, to become a missionary and exile for Christ. He arrived in France in 591. At this time France was ruled by the inefficient Merovingian kings and the country was in a constant state of war and disturbance. The clergy were worldly and most of the population was Christian in name only. With the permission of the king of Burgundy, Columbanus and his companions settled in Annegray in the Vosges mountains and began to preach the Gospel. But so great was the number of followers attracted by the Irishmen that a new and larger monastery had to be established in Luxeuil.

When a new king succeeded to the throne, Columbanus fell into a dispute with him and he was expelled and placed aboard a ship bound for Ireland. However, he escaped, and with his companions he made his way up the Rhine and wished to settle near Lake Constance in Switzerland. Here he met fierce hostility from the pagans. Leaving St Gall behind, Columbanus and his companions crossed the Alps into Italy in 612. In the Apennine mountains he founded his famous monastery, Bobbio, and here he died in November 615.

Columbanus was not only Ireland's greatest missionary to Europe. He was also a scholar and a writer. He studied the Bible and the Fathers of the Church, but he also read Horace, Virgil and the other great pagan authors. He himself was one of the great Latin writers of his time. He was the correspondent and adviser of popes and kings and was one of the leading European churchmen of his day. He was responsible for a great growth in the number of monasteries, and many of the founders of later monasteries were trained at Luxeuil and followed a rule written by St Columbanus himself. It was he who introduced the practice of frequent private confession to the Church.

Above all, he was the first and greatest of the Irish missionaries to Europe.

Statue of St Kilian on the old bridge over the Main at Würzburg. In the background is the castle of the bishops of Würzburg.

The shrine in which the relics of the Irish saint, Dymphna, are preserved in Gheel, Belgium.

The Irish Mission to France and Switzerland

St Gall, whom St Columbanus left behind in Switzerland, lived first as a hermit. Later, he gathered a group of monks about him and preached the Gospel to the pagan Alemans. He died about 650. About 720, a monastery, following the ideals of St Columbanus, was founded where St Gall had lived and this became one of the great European centres of Irish influence.

From about 650, Irish missionaries poured into Europe. Their lively faith, their austerity and their learning were well known, and soon won them followers. They found powerful protectors among the nobility and they and their disciples founded monasteries all over northern and eastern France.

One of the great Irish centres in Europe was Péronne which was known as 'Péronne of the Irish'. This part of France had long been under Irish influence, but it was the mission of three brothers, Fursa, Foillán and Ultán, which made Péronne famous. Fursa arrived in England about 630 and founded the monastery of Burgh Castle in Suffolk. About ten years later he crossed over to France and founded a monastery near Paris. He died about 650 and he was buried at Péronne. His brother, Foillán, then brought his monks to Péronne, and after his departure the third brother, Ultán, became Abbot of Péronne. Péronne became a great centre of Irish pilgrimage and it remained a place of Irish influence until it was destroyed by the Norse in 880.

The Irish Mission to Germany

In the seventh century the German land east of the Rhine—Thuringia, Franconia, Swabia and Bavaria—were for the most part pagan. But in the seventh and eight centuries they were converted to Christianity by Irish monks and by monks trained in Irish schools, who followed the ideals of St Columbanus. Indeed, the monastery of St Columbanus at Luxeuil played an important part in the conversion of the Germans. St Kilian and

The Irish mission to Germany continued into the later middle ages. Above, the 'Irish Door' of the church of St James, Regensburg, which was an Irish Benedictine monastery from the twelfth to the sixteenth century.

his companions became the apostles of Thuringia and Franconia. In 689 he and two of his disciples were martyred at Würzburg. His tomb became a place of pilgrimage and Würzburg became a centre of Irish influence in Germany.

Another Irishman, Fergal or Virgilius, who had been Abbot of Achadh Bó in Ossory, left Ireland about 742 and worked as a missionary in Bavaria. He eventually became Bishop of Salzburg. He worked particularly among the pagan Slavs of Carinthia where he had a successful mission. He died in 784. Fergal was a man of the widest learning. He taught the existence of the antipodes and he wrote one important work which contains his theories about the earth and some interesting geographical information.

Irish Scholars and Teachers

When Charles the Great became ruler of France he made many important reforms, especially in the education of the clergy. He reorganized the palace school and he appointed the famous English scholar, Alcuin, as master of the school. Between 787 and 789 he ordered that all bishops and all monasteries should maintain a school to educate the clergy and teach Latin. Throughout his reign and throughout the reign of his son Louis the Pious (814–40), France became a great centre of learning which attracted many foreign scholars. From the beginning, Irish scholars played a very important part in this revival of learning. They were attracted by the patronage of the French emperors and came in great numbers. However, many of them were refugees, fleeing before the pagan Vikings who began their attacks on Ireland in 795. These men were not preachers and missionaries like their predecessors, but teachers and men of learning.

Alcuin's successor as master of the palace school was an Irishman, Clement, who wrote a valuable book on Latin grammar. Another Irish scholar, Dúngal of St-Denis, who was

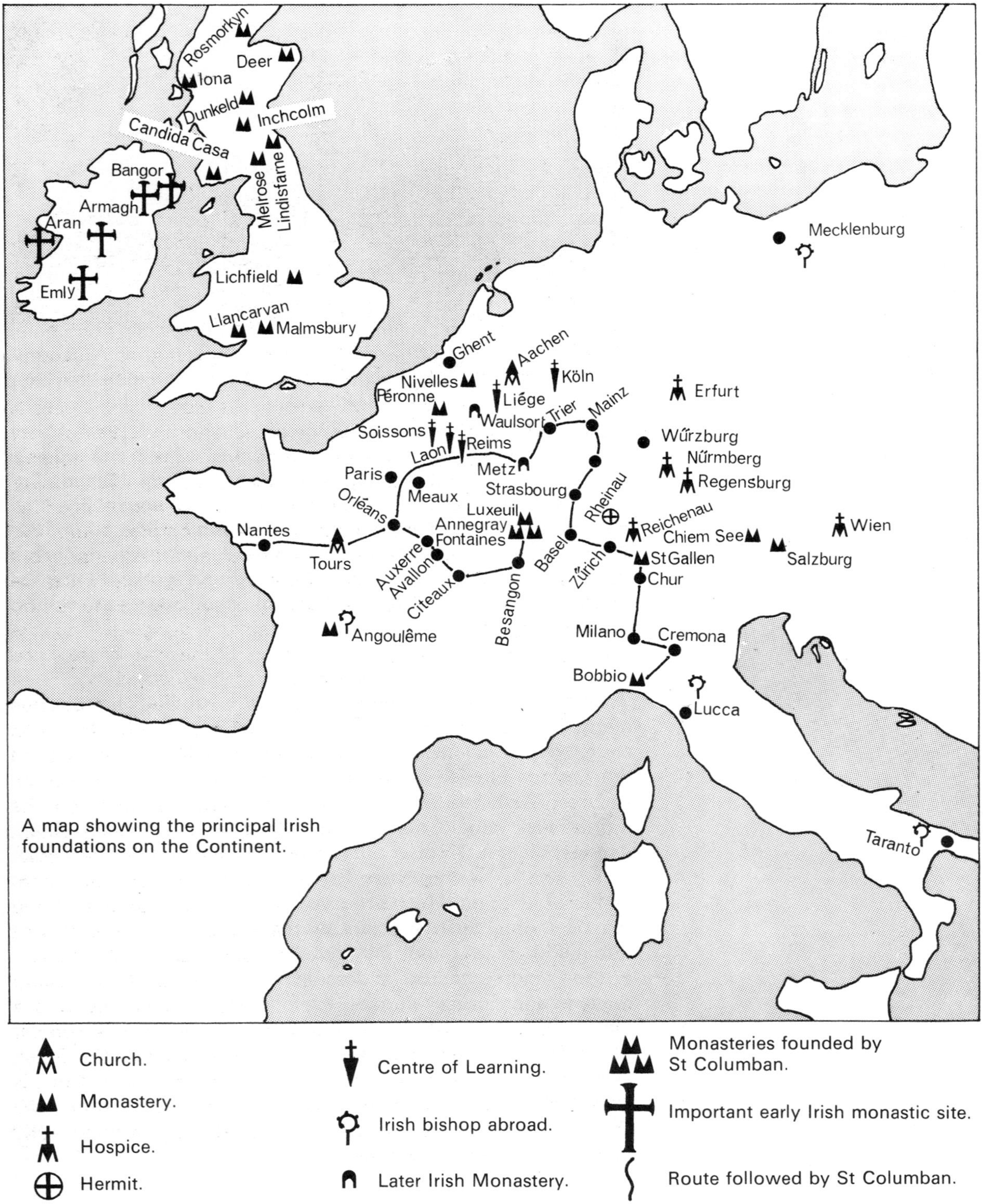
Rosmorkyn
Deer
Iona
Dunkeld
Inchcolm
Candida Casa
Melrose
Lindisfarne
Bangor
Armagh
Aran
Emly
Lichfield
Llancarvan
Malmsbury
Mecklenburg
Ghent
Aachen
Köln
Nivelles
Péronne
Liége
Erfurt
Waulsort
Trier
Mainz
Soissons
Laon
Reims
Würzburg
Nürnberg
Metz
Paris
Regensburg
Meaux
Strasbourg
Orléans
Rheinau
Luxeuil
Annegray
Fontaines
Reichenau
Wien
Nantes
Chiem See
Tours
Auxerre
Avallon
Basel
St Gallen
Salzburg
Zürich
Chur
Citeaux
Besançon
Angoulême
Milano
Cremona
Bobbio
Lucca
Taranto
Church.
Monastery.
Hospice.
Hermit.
Centre of Learning.
Irish bishop abroad.
Later Irish Monastery.
Monasteries founded by St Columban.
Important early Irish monastic site.
Route followed by St Columban.
A map showing the principal Irish foundations on the Continent.

Devotion to Irish saints continues on the Continent. Above, the church of St Colman, an Irish pilgrim to the Holy Land, murdered at Stockerau, near Vienna at the beginning of the eleventh century.

active from about 784 to 827, wrote an account of the eclipse of the sun in 810 for the Emperor, Charles. We know very little of the life-story of Diciul, another Irishman at the imperial court, who was one of the greatest scholars of his day. He was probably a monk of Iona who came to the Continent about 806. He was well-known at the court in 814 and he died some time after 825. He wrote works on grammar and astronomy, but his most important work is a book on geography, *Liber De Mensura Orbis Terrarum*, 'the best book on geography during the Middle Ages'. This book contains a geography of the world, but it also contains an account of the Irish monks and hermits who journeyed to the Faroes and to Iceland.

One of the most learned men of his time, Sedulius Scottus (Sedulius the Irishman) arrived in Liège about 848. He was a theologian, a philosopher, a poet and a scholar. He had a good knowledge of Greek, a rare thing in those days. He wrote some of the finest Latin poetry of his time, commentaries on the Scripture, and a work called *On Christian Rulers*, which describes the duties of a king and how he should rule his people.

In Laon, a distinguished group of Irish scholars, of whom Johannes Scottus Eriugena was the greatest, taught at the palace school. Eriugena arrived there about 845 and taught about 870. According to one scholar, except for St Columbanus, Eriugena was 'the most important individual that Ireland gave to Continental Europe in the Middle Ages'. He was a master of the Latin language and the greatest Greek scholar of his day. He translated many important works from the Greek and wrote commentaries on them and on the Bible. But his chief claim to fame is his work on philosophy, *Concerning the Division of Nature*, which is the first great work of philosophy produced in Western Europe.

Things to Do

1. Draw a map of Europe and mark in the most important Irish monasteries.
2. Why was the Irish mission to Europe so important and what did Irish missionaries and teachers achieve on the continent?
3. Compare the work of St Columcille and St Columbanus. Which was the more important?

Books to Read or Consult

L. Bieler, *Ireland: Harbinger of the Middle Ages,* London 1963.
T. Ó Fiaich, *Gael-scrínte i gcéin,* Dublin 1961.
Frank MacManus, *Saint Columban,* Dublin 1963.

Life in Ireland in the Seventh and Eighth Centuries

Ornamental capitals from the Book of Kells.

Kings and Kingdoms

In Ireland in the seventh and eighth centuries there were between 100 and 150 petty kingdoms, each ruled by its own king. Several of these petty kingdoms joined together made up an overkingdom which was ruled by a *ruiri* or overking. Over and above all these kingdoms were the five provincial kings. Of the provincial kings, the most powerful were the kings of Tara and the kings of Cashel.

The Uí Néill kings of Tara had gradually extended their authority. They conquered a great portion of western and southern Ulster and they drove the Leinstermen out of the plain of Meath. By about 600 the Uí Néill kings at Tara were the most powerful kings in Ireland. Soon, they and their supporters claimed that they were kings of all Ireland, but this was an empty boast. Even after hundreds of years of war, the Uí Néill kings failed to conquer Leinster, Connacht resisted them, and Munster remained completely independent of them.

The Eoganacht kings at Cashel governed Munster, the largest and richest of the provinces. They were second in power only to the Uí Néill kings. Indeed, Cathal mac Finguine, king of Munster who died in 742, was the most powerful king of his day and the Munsterman claimed that he compelled the king of Tara to submit to him.

Men pulling each other's beards, an ornamental capital from the Book of Kells.

A ringfort, the ordinary dwelling-place of a prosperous early farming family.

Lords and Commons

The Irish nobles were land owners who drew rents from their clients or tenants. They did little or no manual work. They represented their families, clients and followers in dealings with the king. They attended on the king and owed him food-rent. Finally, they made up the most important part of the king's army in time of war.

The clients were freemen who did the work, tilled the soil and paid their rents. A noble's status depended on the number of clients he possessed. There were two types of clients: free clients and base clients. The lord gave the free client stock to graze his land in return for a fixed rent. The base client received stock from his lord as well as a large additional payment. In return, he paid his lord a food-rent and he had to provide a certain amount of labour for his lord at harvest time and on other occasions. In addition, the lord defended his clients against violence from others. The client remained a free man and he could change lords if he wished.

The free client was usually a comfortable farmer who held a few hundred acres of land, twenty milch cows, oxen, pigs, sheep and a horse. He owned all his own farm equipment, had full legal rights and enjoyed a comfortable standard of living.

This artificial island in a midland lake is believed to have been a crannóg.

Homes and Houses

There were no towns in Ireland at this period. Indeed, the nearest thing to a town was the large monastic settlement with its monks, scholars, and large monastic farms and workshops. As in earlier times, the homes of the people were isolated and scattered throughout the countryside. The homes of rulers and wealthy farmers were surrounded by a *ráth* or high bank of earth or stone, sometimes mounted on a palisade. The houses of important rulers were surrounded by two or three banks and were more elaborately defended. There are over 30,000 ráths in Ireland, but of course, not all houses were defended by a ráth. The ráth was not usually for defence in

Severe penalties for trespass were laid down in early Irish law. The law also laid down the kind and size of fences to be used. This drawing shows you what the fences of the early Irish farmers looked like.

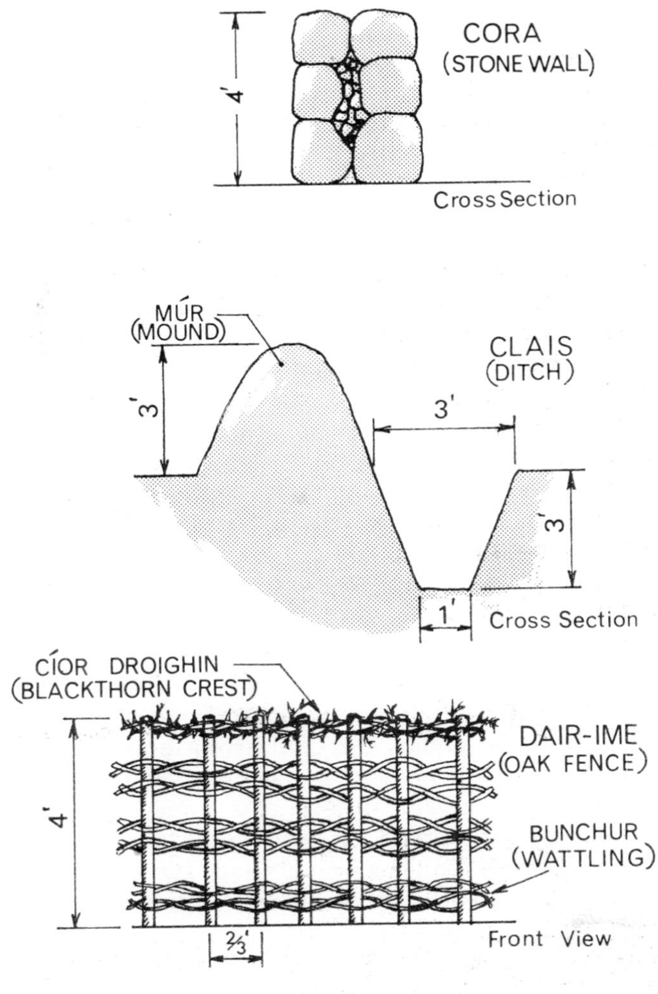

Butter-making was always an important part of Irish life. This wooden churn, twenty-one inches high, was discovered at Lissue, Co. Antrim.

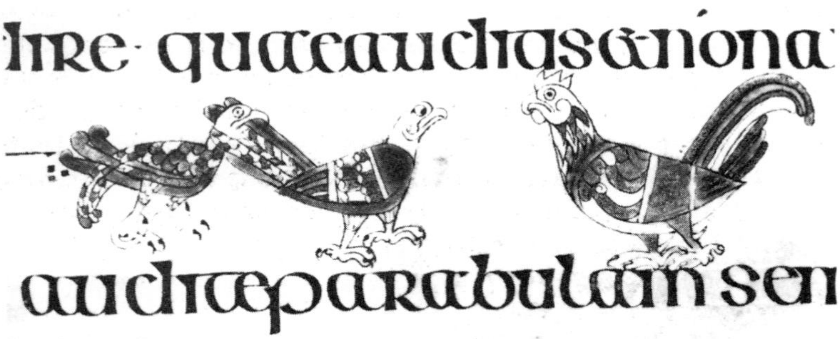

Farmyard fowl, from interlined drawings in the Book of Kells.

war, but for protection against wild animals, cattle-raiders and thieves. It is likely that cattle were driven inside the ráth at night-time. Many ráths have underground passages and artificial caves which were used as places of refuge in times of danger and storage space for grain and other goods in time of peace. Within the enclosure stood the houses and domestic buildings. The houses were round, made of wood and thatched with reeds or rushes. Where wood was scarce, stone was used as a building material. Some houses were rectangular in shape and slates or shingles were sometimes used in roofing. In the centre of the houses stood the hearth, and when the fire was lit the smoke escaped through a hole in the roof. By our standards the houses, both of lords and peasants, were extremely dirty and reeked with smoke and the smell of refuse and waste which accumulated on the floor. Instead of cleaning out the rubbish, the house-holders laid down a new clay floor and the process began again. In the north and north-west of Ireland, where there are many small lakes, important rulers lived in *crannógs* or lake-dwellings. The crannóg was an artificial island built in a lake with timber, stone and clay. A wooden palisade was then erected around it and houses were built inside the palisade. The island was approached by a winding underwater causeway or by boat.

Farmyard fowl, from interlined drawings in the Book of Kells.

Farming

At this period, Irish farmers were mostly cattle-farmers. All prices were reckoned in terms of cattle, and a man's wealth was counted in cattle. The cattle were grazed in the outland pastures in summer, and the people lived off their produce—milk, butter, cream, cheese and curds. In winter, many of the cattle were killed off, and beef, together with bread and porridge was the chief winter food. The cattle were similar in breed to the cattle we have today, though they were smaller in size. Pigs, sheep and goats were also kept. The infield —the land about the dwelling-house—was tilled. From about

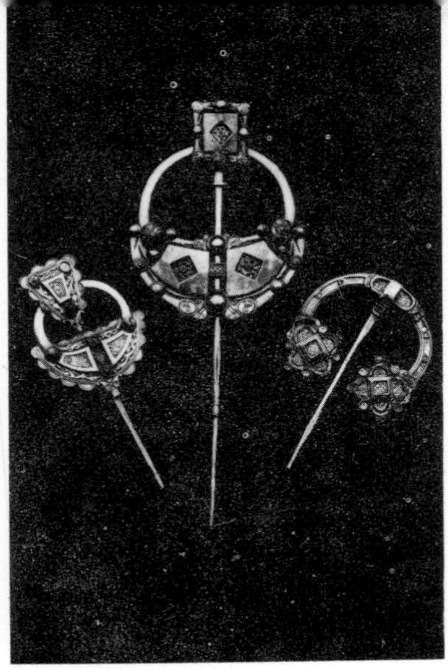

Three silver ring-brooches with ornamented panels of gold. *Left:* from Roscrea, Co. Tipperary, eighth century A.D.; *centre:* from Killamery, Co. Kilkenny, about 850 A.D.; *right:* from Kilmainham, Dublin about 800 A.D.

the time of the introduction of Christianity a new and heavier type of plough, drawn by oxen, was used. In the seventh and eighth centuries there was a big expansion in agriculture and much new land was brought under the plough. The chief grain-crops grown were wheat, oats and rye. The corn was reaped with bill-hooks and sickles. The grain was dried in corn-drying kilns and ground on querns or in large water-mills. Flax for linen-making was also grown.

Food and Drink

Dairy products were the chief food in summer; beef, bread and porridge in winter. A great deal of pork and salt bacon was also eaten. Bee-keeping was an important activity and honey a favourite food. On the sea-coast and by the lakes and rivers, fish formed an important part of the diet. The salmon was the most prized of all fish, but trout, sea-fish and shell-fish—limpets, periwinkles, scallops and oysters—were eaten in large quantities. The Irish supplemented their diet by hunting and fowling. The bones of deer, wild geese and wild duck have been found on the sites of ancient dwellings. Leeks,

A plaque of the crucifixion from Clonmacnoise. It dates from the eighth to the tenth century.

dulse and other vegetables were eaten and nuts, apples, and wild berries were collected. Meat was boiled in great bronze or iron cauldrons or roasted on a spit over the fire. Food was also cooked out of doors. Large wooden or stone cooking-troughs were filled with water. The meat was then placed in the cooking-troughs. A fire was lit, large stones were heated in the fire and then dropped into the water, which soon came to the boil and cooked the meat.

A mounted figure from the shaft of a stone cross at Banagher, Co. Offaly. It dates from about 800 A.D.

A drawing of a man on horseback from the Book of Kells.

Crafts and Trades

Metal-working was carried on all over the country. Beautiful objects—shrines, reliquaries, sacred vessels and croziers for the clergy and ornaments and brooches for the lay people—were produced by Irish craftsmen. Copper smelting and bronze-work and the production of iron tools and weapons continued and we have evidence that glass-making was carried on. Carpenters had a high measure of skill, both in building crannógs and in wood-carving for decorative purposes. The carpenters had saws, chisels, hammers, adzes and awls. Coopers produced wooden drinking vessels, storage vessels and churns. There is little evidence for pottery. Most of the pottery found in the south of Ireland was imported by those engaged in the wine trade. In the north, cooking pots and saucepans were produced by native potters, but these were not of a very high standard.

A deer caught in a deer-trap from the shaft of a stone cross at Banagher, Co. Offaly. It dates from about 800 A.D.

Travel and Trade

Kings travelled with their retinue and were entertained by their subjects in winter-time. When the provincial king was appointed he made a circuit of his province to receive the

A hound catching a hare, from the Book of Kells.

A seated figure with a harp, from the shrine known as the Breac Maedhóic which dates from the eight to the eleventh century.

Figure of a seated harper from the high cross at Moone. It probably represents King David playing his harp.

submission of the lesser kings. Poets and entertainers travelled widely and clerics went on pilgrimage or on visitation of churches and monasteries. But like the people of most countries in the early Middle Ages, the average Irishman of his day travelled very little. Most of the necessities of life were produced in his own area and he had little need to go further afield.

According to tradition, five great roads led to Tara, and there are accounts in old texts of other roads. Most of them seem to have been no better than cattle-tracks or pathways suitable for travel on horseback. People also travelled in carts drawn by one or two horses. Many people travelled by river and lake in curraghs or in various types of timber built boats. Dugout canoes were also used.

There were few if any markets in Ireland. At the *óenach* or assembly of the people of one petty kingdom, a certain amount of trading was carried on, but the óenach never took place more than once a year and was not intended to be a market. A certain amount of overseas trade was carried on, especially the wine trade with France which was important in the south of Ireland. At this time Ireland had no coinage and all trade was carried on by barter or exchange. All prices, fines and payments were reckoned in terms of cattle.

The story of the conversion and death of King Lóegaire from the Book of the Dun Cow. Lóegaire was one of the early historical kings of Tara.

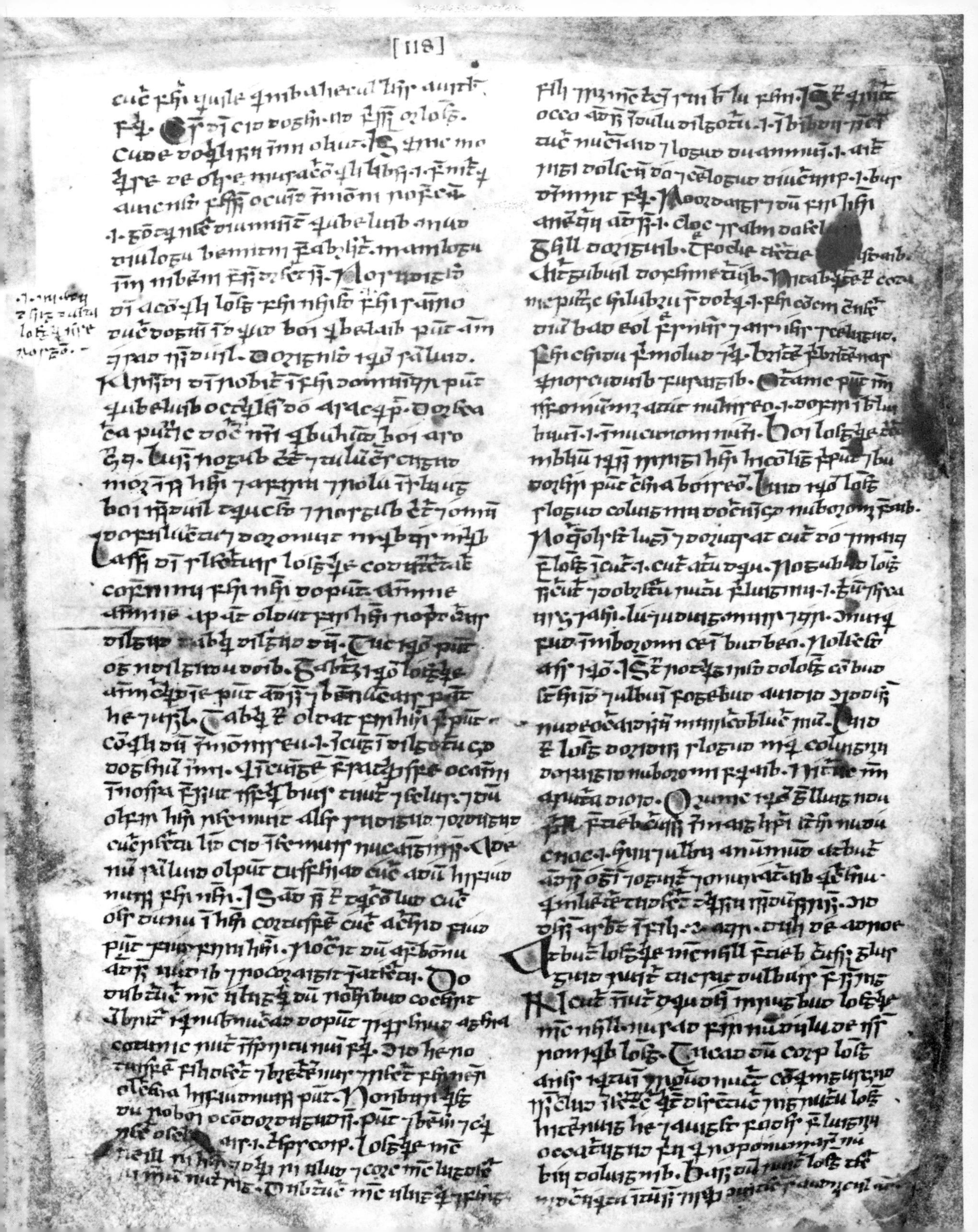

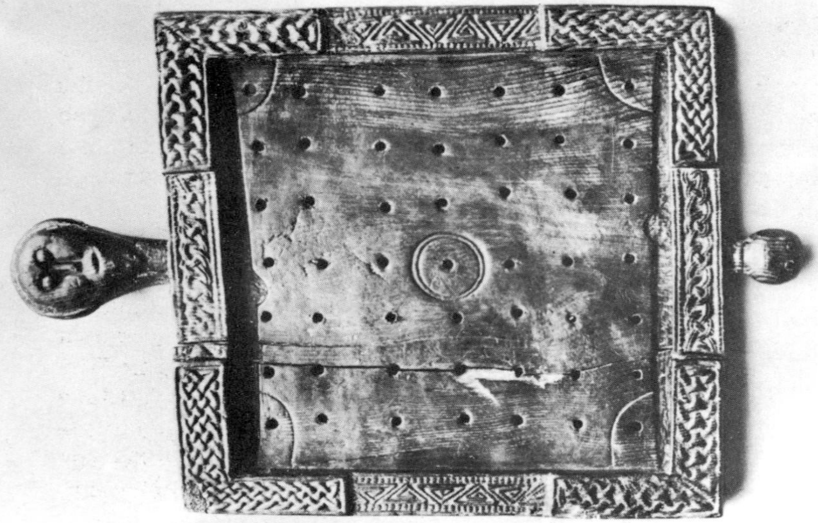

A gaming board made of yew for playing a game with pegs. It dates from the tenth century and was found in a crannóg at Ballinderry, Co. Westmeath.

Entertainments

Next to cattle-raiding, which was as much a sport as a method of warfare among the nobles, the deer-hunt, the boar-chase and fowling were the favourite activities. Horse races took place on the green outside the royal ráth. A form of hurling was played by young men and there are accounts in the old tales of the pleasure the kings and nobles took in watching the play. At the óenach or assembly of the people, where laws were passed and other official business done, time was devoted to games and entertainment. Minstrels, timpanists and entertainers were present.

Indoors, the Irish played board games called *fidchell* and *brandub*, which may have resembled chess or draughts. They also played games of dice. Harpists, bards, jugglers, buffoons and satirists entertained the company at feasts. The favourite instrument was a small harp which rested on the knee while the harpist plucked the strings with his long nails. The harpist accompanied the bard when he recited poems in the presence of the king and nobles. The lower classes seem to have played flutes and bagpipes.

Storytelling seems to have been the most popular pastime of all classes, as it is in the Gaeltacht to the present day. The *story-teller* was able to recite a wide variety of tales. In the seventh and eighth centuries many of these tales were written down and preserved in manuscripts. They make up a great part of early Irish literature.

Literature

One of the earliest collections of Old Irish literature was the Book of Drumsnat which was written in the first half of the eighth century. It contained some very early tales and an account of the history of Ireland. This book was later lost, but most of its contents and a huge collection of other tales were copied into other manuscripts and preserved.

There are four main groups of tales in early Irish literature:

1. *The Mythological Tales*. These are the tales of the ancient Irish gods. The most important story is 'The Battle of Moytirra' which tells how the Irish gods did battle against their enemies, the Fómuiri. Other interesting tales are 'The Dream of Óengus' and 'The Wooing of Étaín'. Many of these tales tell of the journeys of human beings to the land of the gods, *Tír na nÓg*, where there is neither age nor sorrow nor sin, but beautiful people and eternal youth.

2. *The Ulster Sagas*. These are the tales of the Ulster heroes, ruled over by Conchobar mac Nessa, who had his capital at Emain Macha, near modern Armagh. The greatest of the warriors is Cú Chulainn and the epic tale *Táin Bó Cualgne* tells how Cú Chulainn defended Ulster single-handed against the armies of the Connachtmen who had come to drive off the famous Brown Bull of Cualgne. This story was probably first written down in the seventh century. In the course of time a whole series of stories grew up about the Ulster heroes. These include 'The Feast of Bricriu', 'The Exile of the Sons of Usnech' (i.e. the story of Deirdre) and many other fine tales.

3. *The Legends of the Kings*. The stories of the kings are amongst the oldest tales in Irish literature. The earliest of them are the stories of the great legendary kings and founders of kingdoms in Ireland. Some of them are origin legends, tales which explain the origin of tribes and kingdoms and which tell how they were founded. Some of the most important of these tales concern Labraid Loingsech, the ancestor of the Leinstermen, Cormac mac Airt, the legendary king of Tara, and Eogan Mór, the ancestor of the kings of Munster. However, legends and stories also grew up about later kings: Rónán, king of Leinster (+624) who slew his son in error; Guaire, King of Connacht who was famous for his generosity; and Suibne king of Dál nAraide, who went mad at the battle of Moira (637) and became a wild bird-man wandering through the woods of Ireland.

4. *The Cycle of Finn*. These are the tales of Finn mac Cumaill and his warrior band. Finn was originally a divine pagan hero, and in the seventh and eighth centuries the ordinary people told tales of adventure and magic concerning him. Later, the learned writers wrote literary tales, poems and ballads about Finn, Oisín, Diarmaid and the heroes of the Fianna. But Finn remained the hero of the peoples' tales and even today you may hear the Gaeltacht *seanchaí* narrate stories of Finn, as his ancestors did more than a thousand years ago.

Things to Do

1. Read a number of the books listed below. Pick out your favourite tale and write an account of it.
2. There are over 30,000 ráths or ring-forts in the country. Make a list of those in your neighbourhood.
3. Arrange a school-outing to a large ráth. Bring along tapes. Measure its width, and the height of the earthen banks. Find out if it has underground caves. When you have done this, write an imaginative account of what life would be like in the ráth in ancient times.
4. Do you think you could have a picnic or barbecue and cook food as the old Irish did? Yes, you could but be very careful.
5. Imagine that you were living in eighth-century Ireland. Write an account of the day's activities and the night's entertainment. Describe the type of house you lived in, the food you had and how it was cooked and what you did for amusement.

Books to Read or Consult

Myles Dillon (ed.) *Early Irish Society*, Dublin 1954.
M. & L. de Paor, *Early Christian Ireland* (Chapter 3), London 1958.
P. W. Joyce, *Old Celtic Romances*, Dublin 1961.
Standish O'Grady, *The Coming of Cuchulainn*, Dublin 1938.
O Floinn and MacCana, *Scéalaíocht na ríthe,* Dublin 1956.
Rosemary Sutcliff, *The High Deeds of Finn Mac Cool,* London 1967.
Rosemary Sutcliff, *The Hound of Ulster*, London 1963.

Ireland and the Coming of the Vikings

A carved head from a Viking ship.

Who Were the Vikings

The people of Scandinavia and Denmark still remained pagan after the rest of western Europe had been converted to Christianity. They inhabited the mountainous and woody countries of Norway, Sweden and Denmark. As yet, they were not united into single nations, but it is possible to distinguish three separate groups—Danes, Swedes and Norse. We shall call them Vikings.

They were a hardy and adventurous race of farmers and sailors, but they were also keen businessmen and traders. Their northern homelands were poor, and due to increasing population they began to raid the richer countries about them for plunder and precious metals. Others turned to raiding and adventure because of family feuds or because of the attempts of their kings to extend their power. The Vikings were superb sailors and master ship-builders who had learned their craft well in the Baltic Sea and in the narrow fiords of Norway. The invention of the keel about 600 A.D. made long ocean voyages safe and made it possible for the Vikings to become a great seafaring power. Their ships were masterpieces of shipbuilding. They were deckless boats, a little over 60 feet long and capable of being propelled by sail or by oars. They were suitable not only for ocean travel but for navigating shallow rivers and lakes. Each ship carried between 40 and 60 men.

A Viking ship, known as the Gokstad ship.

Portion of a Viking ship showing the rudder by which it was steered.

The Raids and Voyages of the Vikings

By the year 800 the Vikings were successfully raiding and plundering most of the European countries. The Swedes turned eastwards to Finland and Russia. From about 850 they were founding trading stations on the Gulf of Finland, Lake Ladoga and along the Volga. They founded the great market city of Novgorod and opened up trading routes down the great Russian rivers to the Black Sea and Constantinople. On the lower Dnieper they founded the powerful Viking kingdom of Kiev.

A Viking ship. Notice the long sweeping lines of the timber-work and the sleek design.

From an early period the Vikings colonized the Orkneys and the Hebrides. When the power of the Picts declined and when Charles Martel destroyed the Frisian navy in the North Sea in 734, there was nothing to prevent them raiding all along the European coastline. In 793 they plundered Lindisfarne on the coast of Northumbria, and in 800 they were raiding the French coast. By 844 they were raiding the ports of Spain, and in 859–60 they plundered the Balearic Islands, raided Pisa, and sailed up the Rhone and the Arno. From about 850 they penetrated deeply into England and France. In England they had great successes and in 1017 the descendant of the Viking raiders, Cnut, became king of all the English. In France the Vikings were granted the duchy of Normandy between 910 and 930, for the kings of France found it impossible to drive them out.

The Vikings turned their eyes also towards the islands of the North Atlantic—the Faröes and Iceland. They first landed in Iceland about 860 and between 870 and 930 they established there a large colony with a population of about 30,000. Greenland was first sighted by sailors from Iceland about 900, but the first successful colony of farmers and fishermen was

The ruins of the monastery of Inismurray, over six miles off the Sligo coast. It was plundered by the Vikings in 807.

set up in Greenland by Erik the Red in 985. The Vikings were now within striking distance of America which was soon sighted by sailors driven off course. Between 1000 and 1010 the east coast of America was partly explored by a number of Viking expeditions. They found the land extremely rich and attractive, but they did not settle there, due to the hostility of the Red Indians.

Ireland and the Viking Raiders

The first recorded Viking raid on Ireland took place in 795, when the Vikings plundered and burned the church on Lambay Island. They plundered Iona in the same year, and again in 801, and yet again in 806, when they killed 68 of the monks. In 807 the Abbot and community of Iona were forced to abandon their monastery and they had a new church built at Kells, in Meath. In 807 the Vikings plundered the monastery of Inismurray, off the Sligo coast; in 819 they plundered Howth and the islands in Wexford harbour; in 821 they raided the great monastery of Bangor. Even the lonely monastery of Skellig, eight miles off the Kerry coast was plundered in 823. Most of the Vikings came from south-western Norway and sailed down the west coast of Scotland to Ireland. They appeared suddenly off the coast, captured their booty swiftly, and disappeared as suddenly as they had come. They attacked the monasteries because these were the only rich centres; there were no towns. And the monasteries were rich in precious metals and in gold and silver ornaments.

Many of the monks fled abroad from the Viking terror bringing with them their precious books. One monk, rejoicing at the great storm blowing, which made the seas impassable, wrote in the margin of his manuscript:

A Viking ornament showing an armed man on horseback. The Vikings sailed up the rivers but they used horses to attack the interior.

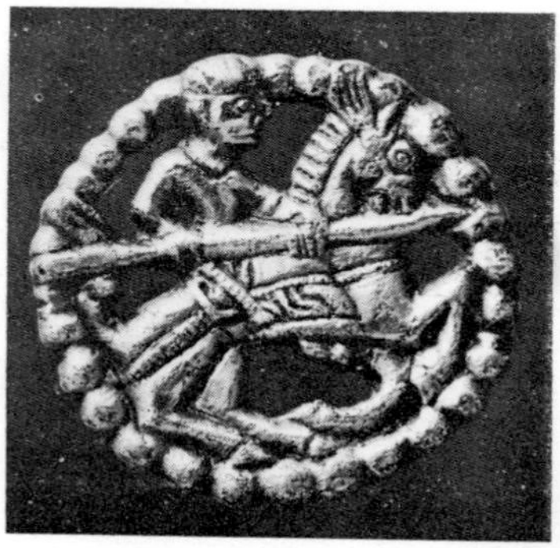

Viking helmets and weapons.

Bitter to-night the wind,
it tosses the sea's white hair;
I'm not afeard of the wild Vikings
coursing on the Irish sea.

Viking Fleets and Settlements

Soon the Vikings encamped on headlands and islands and sailed up the rivers and lakes and into the heart of the country, as they did in England and France. For the Vikings the Shannon was the great gateway into the centre of Ireland. Great fleets began to appear. In 837 the Vikings had 60 ships on the Boyne and 60 on the Liffey. In 841 they made permanent settlements in Dublin and at Annagassan, Co. Louth.

A Viking called Turges made Limerick and the Shannon his headquarters and he plundered deep into the midlands. He led a great fleet into the north, and he had ships on Lough Neagh and Lough Ree. In 845 Meath and Connacht were plundered and the monasteries of Clonmacnoise, Clonfert and Terryglass were burnt. Turges himself captured Armagh. But the Irish leaders united under the Uí Néill king, Malachy I. They captured and drowned Turges and defeated the Vikings in a number of important battles.

Dublin

Dublin, which was founded in 841, became a very important Viking centre. Other towns, Wicklow, Wexford, Waterford, Cork and Limerick, were founded later, but Dublin remained the richest and most powerful of the Viking cities. In 853 the great Viking

A ceremonial Viking cart.

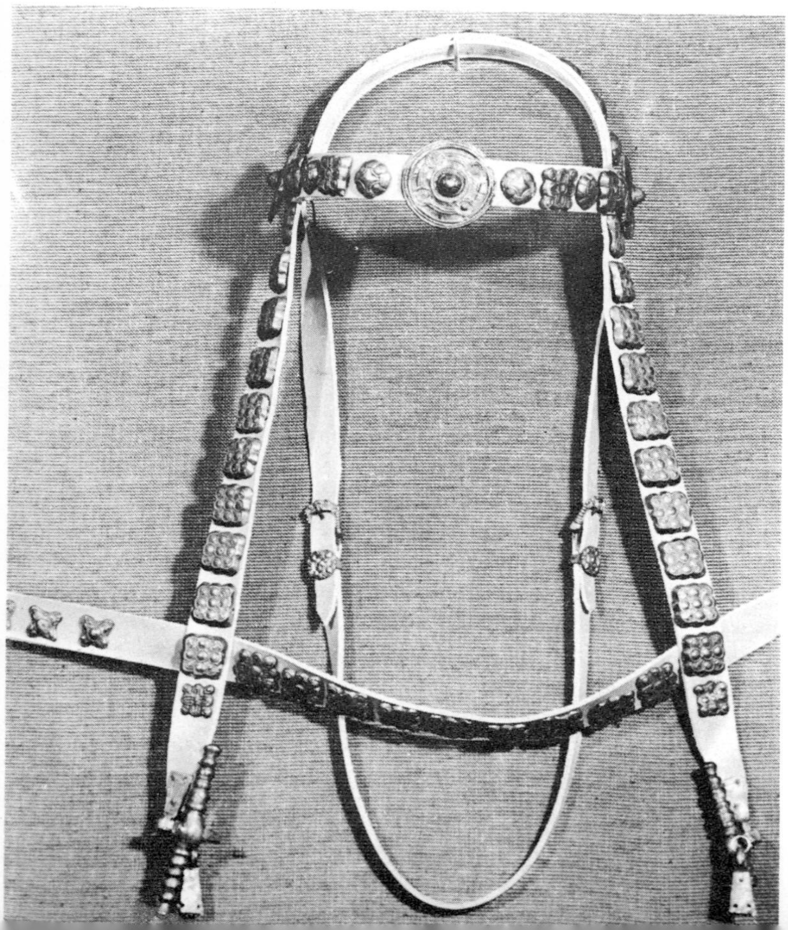

An ornamented Viking bridle.

An Irish warrior, a drawing in the Book of Kells.

leader, Olaf the White, arrived in Dublin. Most of the Irish Vikings submitted to him, and he made himself king of Dublin. Under Olaf Dublin became a prosperous city from which the Vikings attacked Scotland, England and the Isle of Man.

The Wars of the Irish Kings

Ireland was still divided into a number of petty kingdoms, sometimes at peace, sometimes at war with each other. No one king was responsible for the defence of Ireland against the Vikings. The Vikings themselves joined in the struggles between the Irish kingdoms, now on one side, now on the other. They also fought bitterly amongst themselves.

In the course of these wars the Uí Néill kings at Tara gradually grew stronger and attempted to enforce their authority over all Ireland. This brought them to war with the second most powerful kingdom in Ireland, Munster, ruled from the Rock of Cashel by the Eoganacht kings. In 854 Malachy I, king of Tara, invaded Munster and compelled its king to submit. In 866 his successor, Áed Finnliath, captured all the Viking strongholds in the north of Ireland, and from that date the Vikings made

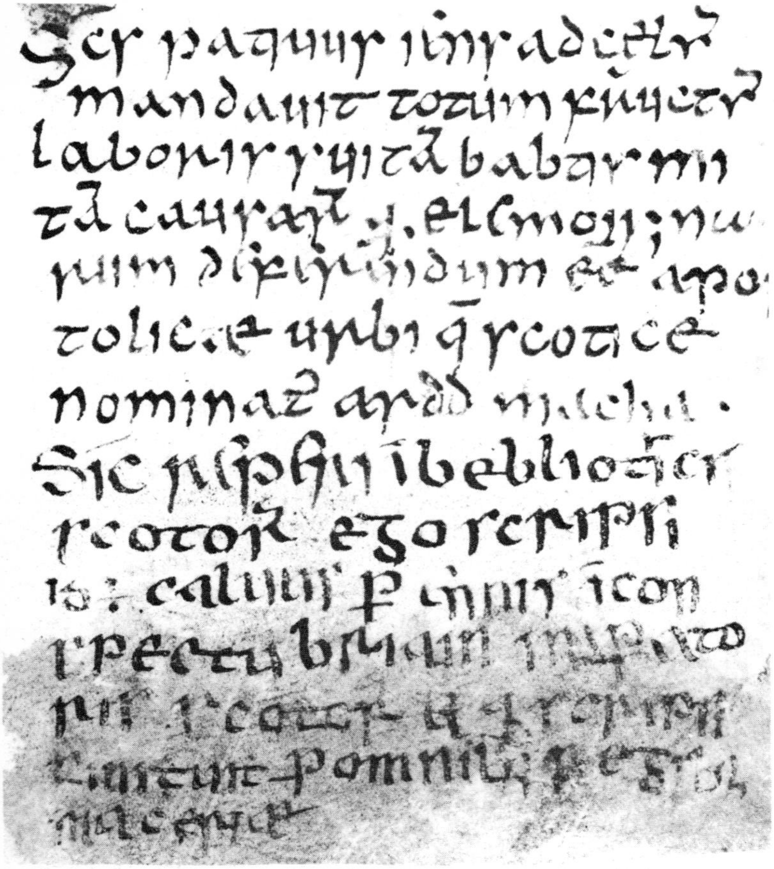

The entry in the Book of Armagh, written at Brian's command, in which he describes himself as Emperor of the Irish.

no settlements north of a line from Dublin to Limerick. The great struggle between Tara and Cashel continued, and the kings of Tara were finally victorious. In 908 Cormac mac Cuillenáin, king of Cashel, was defeated and slain by the king of Tara, Flann Sinna. After this defeat the power of the Eoganacht kings of Cashel faded rapidly.

The Munster Vikings and the Rise of the Dál Cais

After the defeat of the Eoganacht in 908 Munster became weak and soon suffered from heavy Viking attacks. In 914 the Vikings founded Waterford, and using this as a base they raided deeply into Munster. About 920 they established themselves in Limerick, which soon became an important city with colonies inland at Thurles and Cashel. It was now clear that the Eoganacht kings, who were divided among themselves, were no longer able to defend Munster. With the decline of the Eoganacht, the Dál Cais, the kings of a small state in east Clare began to grow powerful. In 964 Mathgamain, the king of the Dál Cais, captured Cashel from the Eoganacht and carried on successful war against the Vikings. Shortly afterwards he

The beautifully preserved round tower at Glendalough.

defeated the Vikings at the battle of Sulchóid and sacked their rich and prosperous city of Limerick. However, in 976 Mathgamain was murdered by the Eoganacht, and his brother, Brian, succeeded him as king of Dál Cais.

The Reign of Brian

Brian was king of Dál Cais in 976 and immediately took the field against his brother's enemies. In 978 he defeated the king of Cashel in battle. Step by step he established himself in the kingship of Munster and fortified the province. He invaded Ossory, took the hostages of the Leinstermen, and forced them to recognize him as overlord. In 983 and again in 988 his fleets ravaged Connacht and plundered Meath. He continued to establish his authority over Connacht and Leinster, and in 997 he compelled the Uí Néill king of Tara, Malachy II to divide the overlordship of Ireland with him.

Malachy II was a powerful and successful king who carried on victorious wars with the Vikings. In 980 he defeated the Dublin Vikings at the battle of Tara and in 981 he besieged and captured their city of Dublin, carried off large booty and placed them under heavy tribute. This practically destroyed the independent power of the Dublin Vikings. The chief struggle now was the struggle for the kingship of Ireland between Malachy II and Brian.

The Leinstermen refused to submit to Brian, and they and the Dublin Vikings rose in rebellion against him. Brian defeated them at Glenn Máma in 999 and in the following year he besieged and burned Dublin. Malachy and his followers now began to fear Brian who clearly aimed at becoming king of all Ireland. From 1001 until 1005 Brian made expedition after expedition into the north until eventually, by a peaceful show of superior power, Brian compelled the northern rulers to submit to him. At last Brian was king of all Ireland, the first high-king, who described himself in the Book of Armagh as 'Emperor of the Irish'.

The round tower at Clonmacnoise.

The Battle of Clontarf

The events leading up to the Battle of Clontarf began when the Leinstermen and the Vikings of Dublin revolted against Brian. The struggle broke out in 1013. Máel Mórda, king of Leinster, allied himself with the Dublin Vikings and went to war with Brian. The struggle soon widened in scope and the Dublin Vikings sought allies overseas. The great Sigurd, Earl of Orkney, came with a large contingent, and the Viking sagas say that the king of Dublin offered Sigurd the kingdom of Ireland. Other Viking contingents came from as far afield as

An artist's impression of the battle of Clontarf.

Iceland and Normandy. Brian gave them battle at Clontarf on Good Friday 1014 and defeated them, but he himself was slain. As the Viking sagas about Clontarf say: 'Brian fell but saved his kingdom. This Brian was the best of kings.' After Clontarf the Viking cities took little part in Irish wars and the Vikings themselves, who had now become Christian, settled down as peaceful traders and merchants.

The Effect of the Viking Wars on Ireland

In the storm and stress of the war, the great Irish kings increased their power and expanded their kingdoms at the expense of the weaker kings. Powerful provincial kingdoms grew up, and the petty kingdoms were reduced or conquered.

Domestic vessels and implements of the Vikings.

A crucifixion plaque from St John's, Rinnagan, Co. Roscommon. It was made during the Viking wars.

Some families, like the Dál Cais, rose to great power and carved out kingdoms for themselves. For the next 150 years the provincial kings were at war with one another for the kingship of all Ireland.

The Vikings founded the first Irish cities. These were prosperous trading ports with markets at home and beyond the seas. When Mathgamain and his followers captured Limerick in 964 they found great wealth there.

> They carried off their jewels and their best property, and their saddles, beautiful and foreign, their gold and their silver; their beautifully woven cloth of all colours and of all kinds. The fort and the good town they reduced to a cloud of smoke and to red fire afterwards.

Dublin, the richest of the Viking cities, had a large trade with Bristol and Wales. It was an important centre of shipbuilding and commerce, with a flourishing slave trade. About 890 coinage was introduced by the Dublin Vikings, and about 995 they began to mint their own silver money. It is clear that Dublin was a great commercial centre and one of the richest cities in western Europe at the time.

Muiredach's cross at Monasterboice, Co. Louth, perhaps the most beautiful and elaborate of all high crosses.

The cross of the Scriptures at Clonmacnoise. The carved panels on the cross depict scenes from the Scriptures.

The earlier Norse raids were responsible for the destruction of many monasteries and the loss of countless books and treasures of art. Many Irish scholars fled abroad to the French schools, bringing their books with them. However, the monasteries of the lower central plain—Clonmacnoise, Terryglass and others—continued to produce Irish literature and fine lyric poetry. During the Viking wars, stone churches began to be built, and round towers, which were designed first as belfries, but later as places of refuge. In this period too, the famous carved high crosses were erected. In general, the Viking wars had an evil effect on the Church and many clerics became worldly. From about 900 the Irish Vikings were becoming Christian and many of them intermarried with the Irish. Olaf Cuarán, king of Dublin, was baptized in 943 and in 980 he went on pilgrimage to Iona and died there 'after penance and a good life'. The coins of Sitric Silkenbeard, king of Dublin (1000–42) bear the sign of the Cross. Sitric made at least one pilgrimage to Rome and he is said to have founded Christ Church Cathedral, Dublin.

Coins of Sitric Silkenbeard, minted at Dublin about 1000 A.D.

Things to Do

1. On a map of Europe mark in the places raided by the Vikings. How were they able to make such long sea-voyages?
2. The Vikings did a great deal of harm in Ireland. What good did they do? Make a list of any benefits they brought Ireland.
3. Why is Brian so important in Irish history?
4. Imagine that you were a Viking watching the battle of Clontarf, from the walls of Dublin. Write an account of the thoughts which ran through your mind.

Books to Read or Consult

J. Brøndsted, *The Vikings*, London 1960.

C. A. Burland, *The Vikings*, London 1961.

Magnusson and Palsson, *The Vinland Sagas*, London 1965: the Vikings' own account of how they discovered America.

Eoin Mac Neill, *Phases of Irish history* (Chapter 9), Dublin 1968.

Peadar Ó Laoire, *Niamh*, Dublin 1907.

Ireland from Clontarf to the Coming of the Normans

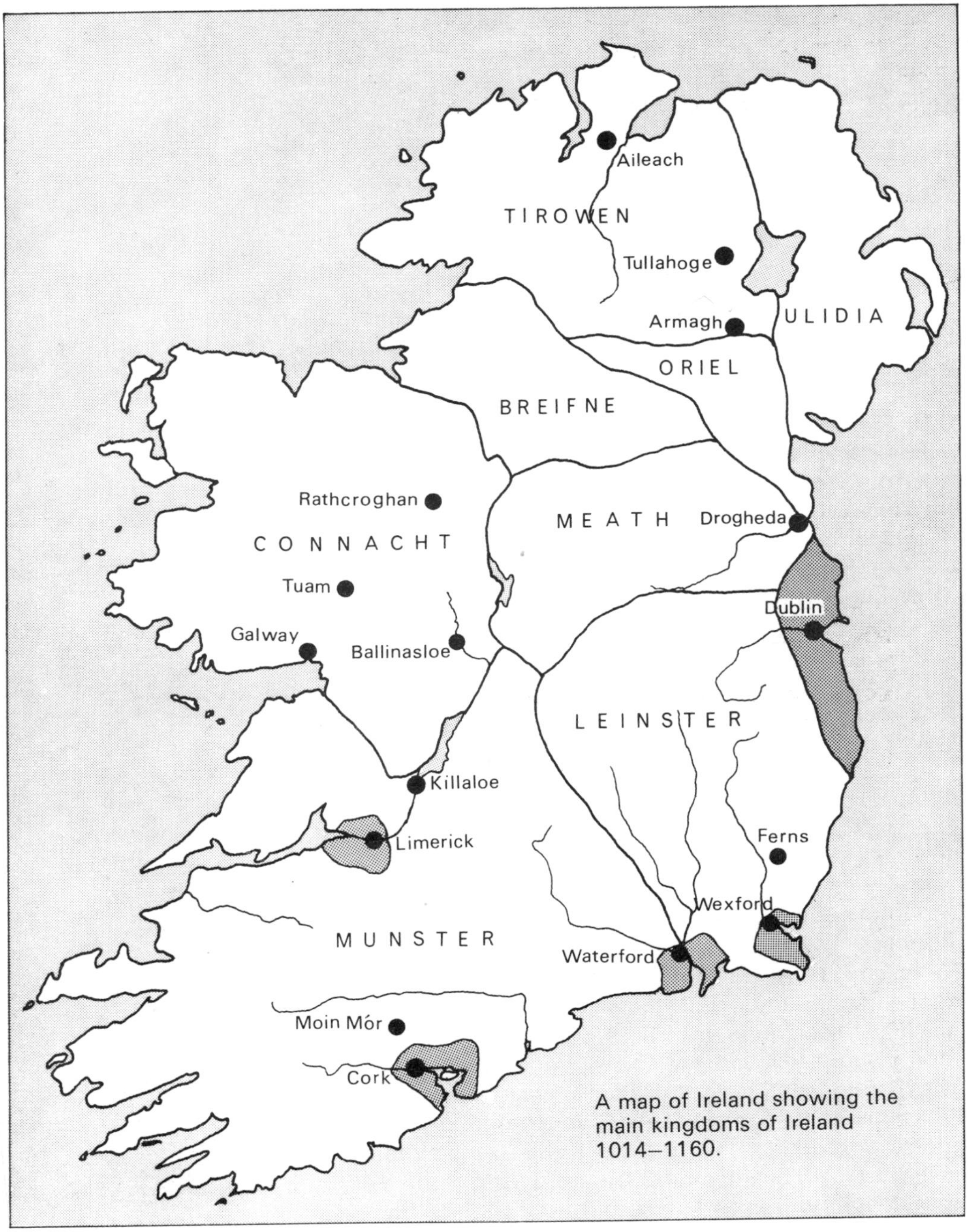

A map of Ireland showing the main kingdoms of Ireland 1014–1160.

Cashel, the ancient seat of the king of Munster, which was handed over to the church by the O'Briens in 1101.

Kings and Kingdoms

During the Viking wars powerful provincial kingdoms grew up in Ireland and these kingdoms waged continuous war against each other for the high-kingship or kingship of all Ireland.

In the south the most powerful kingdom was Munster, ruled by the descendants of Brian. The O'Briens ruled Munster from their palace at Kincora, but they also lived at Killaloe and, later, in the Norse city of Limerick. Cashel, the ancient seat of the kings of Munster, was handed over to the Church in 1101 by Murtough O'Brien. The MacCarthys, the descendants of the Eoghanacht kings of Munster, were the chief rivals of the O'Briens, and they sometimes succeeded in making themselves kings of Munster.

Connacht was ruled by the O'Connors, and for a long time it was the most powerful of the provincial kingdoms. In ancient times, the kings of Connacht ruled from Rathcroghan, but now the O'Connors made Tuam and Galway their capitals. Turlough O'Connor lived in Tuam and in Roscommon, and in 1124 he built castles at Ballinasloe and on the mouth of the Corrib, where Galway now stands. His son, Rory, built a large castle at Tuam in 1164. The most powerful sub-kingdom of Connacht was Brefne, in the north-east of Connacht, which was ruled over by the O'Rourkes.

The most powerful kingdom in the north was the kingdom of Tír Eogain, now ruled by the MacLochlainns. The ancient residence of the kings of Tír Eogain was the great stone fort at Aileach, near Derry. In 1101 Murtough O'Brien invaded the north and destroyed the fort of Aileach. Afterwards, the kings of Tír Eogain lived at Tullahoge, near Lough Neagh, and this became their capital. There were three powerful sub-kingdoms in the north. To the west was the kingdom of Tír Conaill, later ruled over by the O'Donnells. East of the Bann and Lough Neagh was the kingdom of Ulidia. To the south,

The cross of Cong. It was made between 1123 and 1136 for Turlough O'Connor to enshrine a relic of the True Cross. It is a processional cross of oak, covered with decorated bronze plates, decorated with panels of gold.

The ruins of the great Cistercian monastery at Mellifont, the first Irish Cistercian abbey.

stretching from Armagh to Drogheda, was the kingdom of Oriel, ruled by the O'Carrolls. The kings of Tír Eogain claimed to rule over all these kingdoms, but they often met with opposition.

The ancient kingdom of Meath passed into decline after the death of Malachy II in 1022 and never recovered. After that it played no part in the wars of the provincial kings. It was often conquered by the kings of other provinces and divided amongst them.

The kingdom of Leinster was ruled by the family of MacMurrough from 1042, when Dermot I made himself king. He ruled from Ferns, and was the most powerful king in Ireland until his death in 1072. He took the Norse city of Dublin, made war on Meath and Munster and defeated the king of Connacht. He was killed in battle against Meath in 1072. After his death, his family held little power and Leinster became the weakest of the provincial kingdoms.

The Wars of the Kings with Opposition

The Supremacy of Munster

Turlough O'Brien, who became king of Munster in 1063, was one of the most powerful kings of his day. He made himself overlord of Leinster and Meath, and in 1073 the king of Connacht submitted to him. But the north of Ireland always resisted him. Though the Pope and the Archbishop of Canterbury addressed him in letters as king of Ireland, he never succeeded in becoming high king.

Murtough O'Brien, his son, had greater success. He became king in 1086. Within two years Leinster had submitted to him, and he was waging successful war against the king of Connacht. His great enemy was Mac Lochlainn, king of Tír Eogain, but in 1101 Murtough led a great army into the north and compelled Mac Lochlainn and all the northern kings to

Loingsech hua [illegible]
ne i Cind maraid [illegible]
[illegible] Muinchis [illegible] mac
oge quieuit in Christo i Cill
Dalua. Cathal mc
Domnaill do marbad de
sib i Cath ... escop
quieuit in Christo hi Mach
ail Brocain. Isin b
liadain si ro gab ri Erend
i n-Alpain uile co robol
[illegible] Crom ... dolig
dib .i. ... indu.
Sacch mor [illegible]
i mbliadain con ... ill
i ... bor comor.

1079 Kl. iii. Enair .xxiii. f.
.i. uiii. ... sechtmogat
& mile o Chott. Crist.

+ Coibdenach Ultach
... & in
... ardech
... quieuit
i ... Conchobur
hua Briain do marb
ad a fill i ... Eo
gan ... gabail rige
... do marb
do marbad fochetoir. Oc; ... nech
hua Briain do gabail
rige Caisil. Hua Lochlaind
... ri Airgiall

domanbad. Domn
sleibe hua Eochada
do ... co
... Tairrd
elbach hua Briain.
Oc; ... hua
Eochada do gabail
rige Caisil. Cend
Faelad hua ...
galaig ri ...
1080 ... dorche. ... fri

Kl. iii. f. ... .xxiiii.
... hua
... quieuit i
...
Cor... do
...
& ... leo do Th
airrdelbach & ...
...
... Slogad la
Tairrdelbach hua
Briain hi ...
...
...
... Da
hua [illegible] do
1081 domarbad. Sacch
Kl. iii. f. ... .u. hu
... Donn sleibe
hua Eochada do g
abail rige Ulad.
Hu ... ri ;

[illegible]
[illegible]
[illegible]
do ...
... Cotue e
... Sl
... Tairrdelbach
... & ... mide
...
... ri Mide
...
Kl. iii. f. ... .xxiii. f.
Bliadain ... sechtmogat ... mile
i chott. Crist. ...
...
Gall ...
... do
marbad ...
... do ...
sleibe hua Eochada.
... & cell ...
... & ...
... cella do lo
... is bliadain. Ri
Ulad do ... in
... hua Briain .i.
Tairrdelbaig. ...
i ...
Dunchad hua ...
...
... quieuit in
Christo.

The doorway of Clonfert Cathedral. This foundation goes back to the tenth and eleventh centuries. The doorway is in the Romanesque style—a new style of architecture introduced during the reform of the church in the twelfth century.

submit to him. He was now high king. However, Mac Lochlainn defeated him in 1103 and after that the power of O'Brien began to fade. The leading place held by Munster was not taken by Connacht.

Turlough O'Connor (1106–1156)

In 1106 at the age of eighteen, Turlough O'Connor became king of Connacht. He was a soldier of great energy who took the field year after year. He was also a man of intelligence who shaped new policies. He strengthened Connacht by building fortifications. He placed a powerful fleet on the Shannon and he built bridges across the river so that he could attack the other provinces swiftly. His policy was one of divide

A page from the Annals of Inisfallen, one of the most famous books of Irish annals. The Annals of Inisfallen were written in the monasteries of Emly and Inisfallen. This page records events in Ireland from 1077 to 1081.

Two details of carvings at Clonfert Cathedral.

and conquer. In 1118 he led a great army into Munster and divided the kingdom between the O'Briens and the MacCarthys. In 1125 he divided Meath into four portions, and in 1127, after trying unsuccessfully to make his son king of Leinster, he divided Leinster into two parts. In 1130 he was practically king of all Ireland, but in 1131 there was a general revolt against him and it took him almost ten years to win back his former power. O'Connor soon had a new and powerful rival, Murtough MacLochlainn, king of Tír Eogain. O'Connor's last great victory was the battle of Móin Mór (1151) where he destroyed the power of the O'Briens. When he died in 1156 his son, Rory, became king of Connacht, but Murtough MacLochlainn was the most powerful king of Ireland.

Murtough MacLochlainn

MacLochlainn steadily built up his power in the north and he was present at the consecration of Mellifont in 1157 as high king. In that year he marched into the south, captured Limerick and again divided Munster. In 1159 he defeated Rory O'Connor at Ardee, and next year he received the hostages of all the chief rulers of Ireland and was recognized as high king. He and his ally, Dermot MacMurrough, king of Leinster, were now at the height of their power. But MacLochlainn had a short reign. About 1164 his own sub-kings began to revolt, and when, in 1166 he broke his solemn oath and blinded the king of Ulidia, there was a general rebellion against him. Rory O'Connor and his ally, Tiernan O'Rourke, king of Brefne, now took the field. Most of the leaders of the north and east joined O'Connor, and MacLochlainn, deserted by his supporters, was slain in a skirmish (1166).

Rory O'Connor

Rory O'Connor now became high king, the last and greatest of the kings. MacLochlainn's friend and ally, Dermot MacMurrough, was the next to fall. MacMurrough had been king of Leinster since 1126. He was a vigorous and ambitious king and a generous patron of the Church. He and Tiernan O'Rourke, king of Brefne, were rivals for the land of Meath, and in 1152 MacMurrough made off with Tiernan's wife, Dervorgilla. While MacLochlainn was high king MacMurrough supported him against O'Connor and O'Rourke. Now, when MacLochlainn was dead, O'Connor and his friends took their revenge. The men of Leinster rebelled against their king, O'Rourke, and his allies invaded Leinster, divided the kingdom and expelled MacMurrough. In 1166 Rory O'Connor was high king and held greater power than any high king who had gone before him. For the first time in her history Ireland seemed to be united under a single king. But this was not to be. In August 1166 Dermot MacMurrough sailed from Ireland in search of Norman allies beyond the sea.

The Reform of the Irish Church

The State of the Church

As we have seen, the Irish Church suffered terribly during the raids and plunderings of the Vikings. But many of the monasteries made a remarkable recovery, especially the greater ones such as Armagh, Lismore, Clonard, Clonmacnoise, Kildare and Glendalough. These greater monasteries again

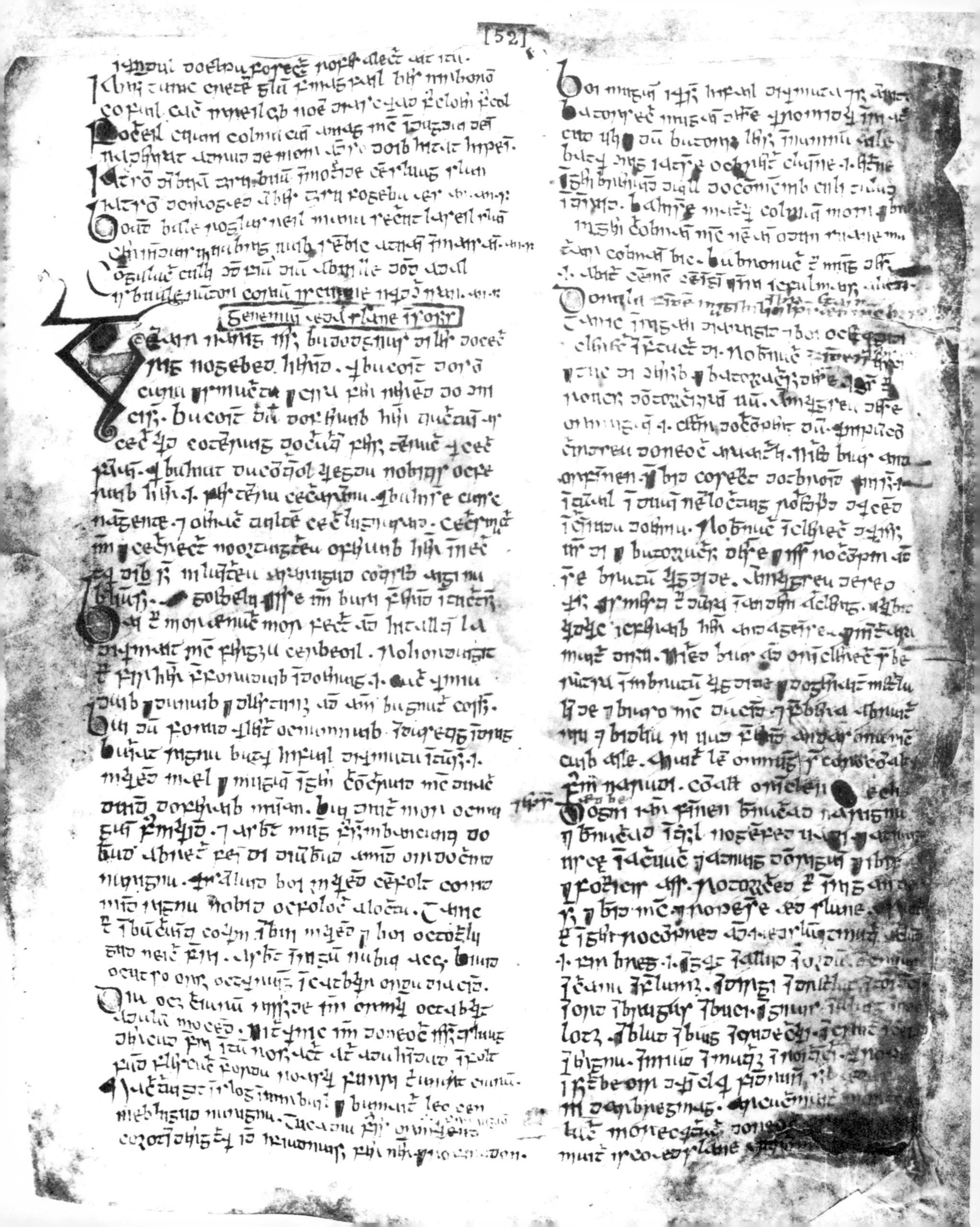

[illegible]

Genemuin Aeda Slane in so

[illegible]

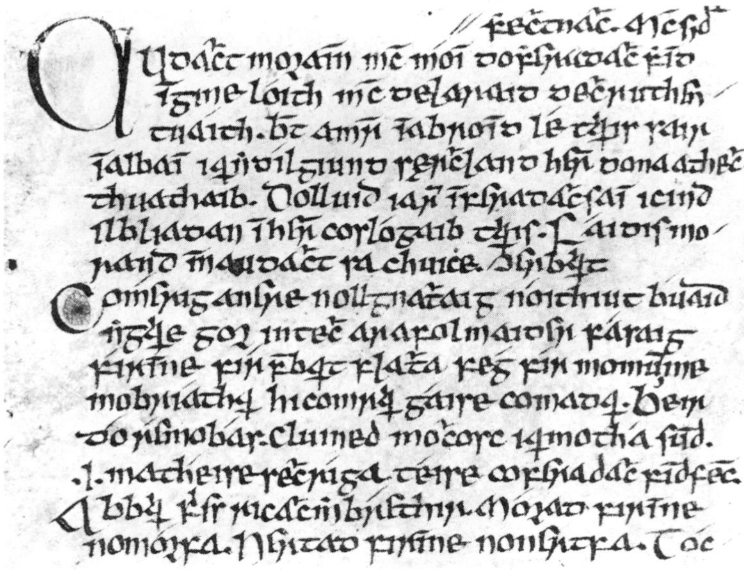

A page from the Book of Leinster, one of the largest collections of Irish history and legend.

became centres of learning and study. However, there were many abuses in the Irish Church. Laymen held office as abbots of monasteries, abbots exercised the powers of bishops, and the country was not divided up into dioceses each ruled by a bishop. Lay people got little or no religious instruction and rarely received the sacraments. Many pagan customs and beliefs survived, and the people followed the pagan Brehon laws of marriage and divorce and did not obey the Church's teaching on marriage.

The Synod of Cashel, 1101

At this time there was a great reform of the Church in progress all over Europe, and it was natural that the movement should spread to Ireland. The Archbishops of Canterbury, Lanfranc, and his successor, St Anselm, wrote to the Irish kings and clergy urging them to reform the Church in Ireland. There was a strong desire for reform amongst some of the Irish clergy, and in 1101 a Synod was held at Cashel, presided over by Murtough O'Brien, the high king and Bishop Ó Dúnáin, the Papal Legate. This Synod passed decrees forbidding simony, lay abbots, marriage of the clergy and marriage within the forbidden degrees of kindred. It also declared that the Church should be free of all rents and tribute.

A page from the Book of the Dun Cow, telling the story of the miraculous birth of Aed Sláine, king of Tara.

The Synod of Ráthbresail, 1111

The first diocese of the modern kind was set up in Dublin about 1030. In 1096 Waterford became a diocese and in 1107

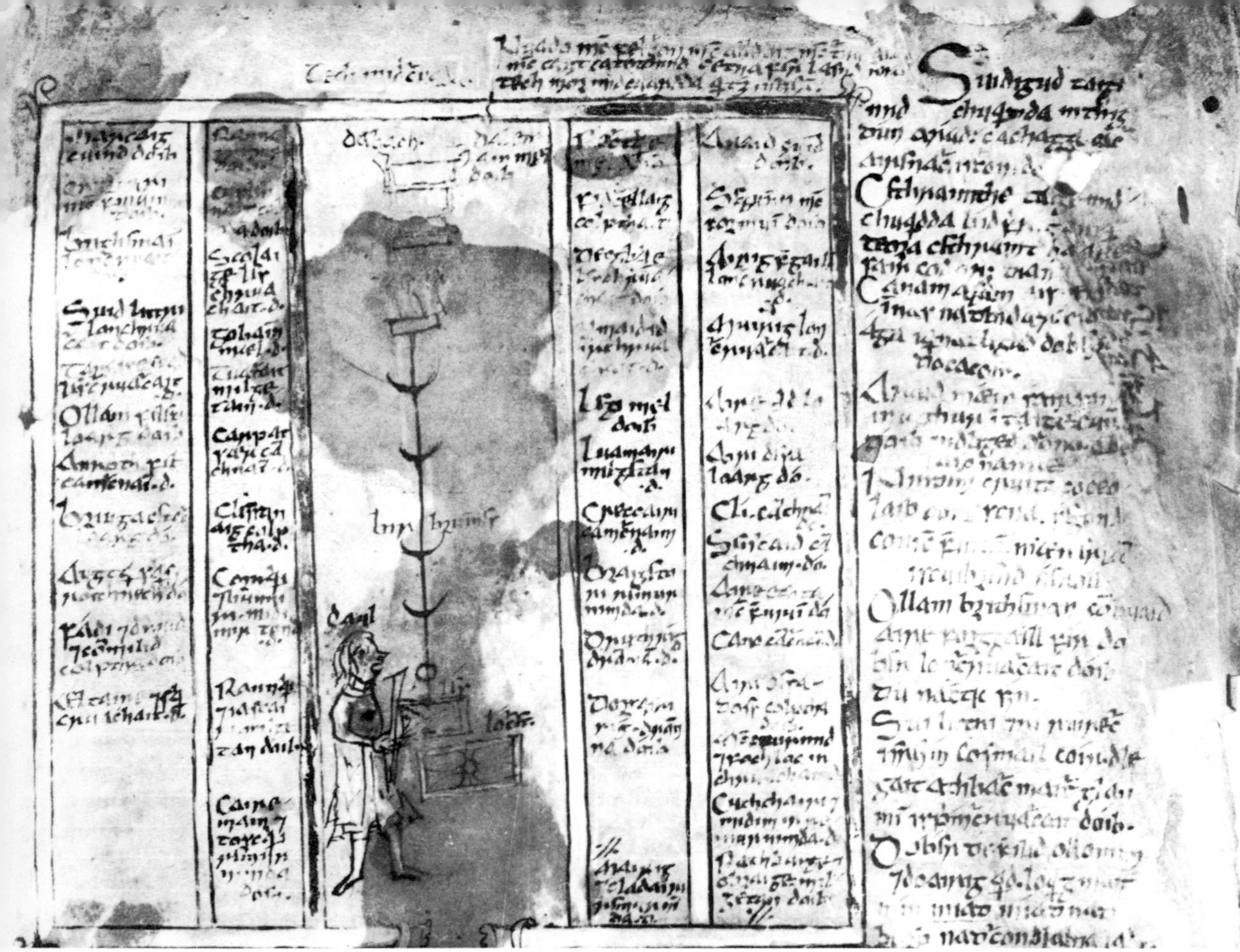

The plan of the banqueting hall at Tara, from the Book of Leinster.

Gilbert was appointed first bishop of the new diocese of Limerick. This Gilbert wrote a book describing how the Irish Church should be reformed. He became Papal Legate, and in 1111 he presided over a second Synod which met at Ráthbresail. At this Synod Ireland was divided into two archbishoprics, Armagh and Cashel, each with twelve dioceses. Now for the first time the Church in Ireland was organized like the Church in Europe.

St Malachy of Armagh (1095–1148)

The greatest of all Irish reformers, St Malachy, was born in 1095, the son of a teacher in the schools of Armagh. He was ordained about 1120 and continued his studies in the famous monastery of Lismore. He returned to Armagh about 1125 and was consecrated Bishop of Connor. Here he began to carry out a great programme of reform, but he was forced to abandon it for a while. In 1132 he was consecrated Archbishop

Cormac's Chapel on the Rock of Cashel, a beautiful Romanesque church built by Cormac MacCarthy and completed in 1134.

The Lismore Crozier. A highly ornamented bronze reliquary made about 1100 A.D. to enshrine the wooden staff of St Mochuda, the founder of the monastery of Lismore, Co. Waterford.

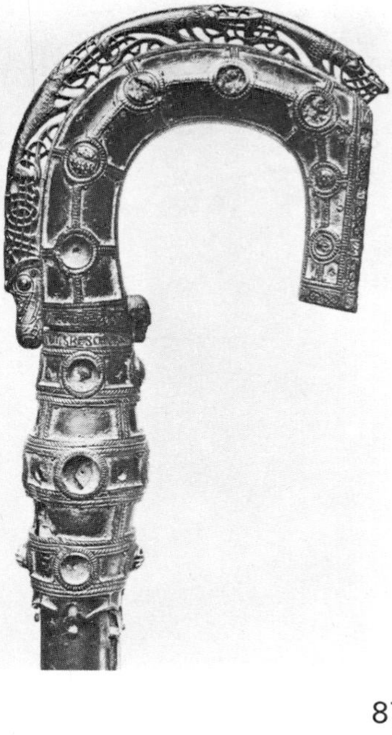

of Armagh, where he carried out important reforms, but in 1137 he resigned and became bishop of the poorer diocese of Down.

In 1139 Malachy set out for Rome to obtain the Pope's approval for the reforms in Ireland and to obtain the grant of the pallium to the Archbishops of Armagh and Cashel. On his way he visited St Bernard at Clairvaux and the two saints became great friends. Malachy greatly admired the Cistercian Order and he left some of his companions at Clairvaux to be trained as Cistercians by St Bernard. These monks, together with some French Cistercians came to Ireland, and in 1141 they founded Mellifont, the first Cistercian abbey in Ireland. Malachy continued his journey to Rome where the Pope approved of the reforms, but he refused to grant the pallia until another synod was summoned. The Pope appointed Malachy Papal Legate and he returned to Ireland to continue the reform. He summoned a Synod, which met at Inis Pádraig, near Skerries, in 1148, and he set out once more for Rome to obtain the pallia. However, he never reached Rome, for he died on the way, at Clairvaux, in the arms of his friend St Bernard.

The Synod of Kells, 1152

The death of St Malachy caused a delay, but in 1150 the Pope sent Cardinal Paparo to Ireland as Papal Legate, and he summoned a Synod to meet at Kells in March 1152. Ireland was

The monastic ruins at Iniscealtra, Co. Clare. The O'Briens were generous patrons of the church at Iniscealtra.

Soiscél Molaise. A bronze reliquary with silver panels and gold ornamentation. It was made about 1000 A.D. for the abbot of Devinish, Co. Fermanagh and it probably contained a copy of the Gospels.

divided into four archbishoprics, Armagh, Cashel, Dublin and Tuam, and 36 Irish dioceses were recognized. The Archbishop of Armagh was declared Primate of Ireland and the cardinal conferred the pallium on the four archbishops. The bishops laid down the Church's marriage law; simony and usury were condemned, and it was decreed that tithes should be paid. A few lesser synods were held before the Norman invasion, but it was the Synod of Kells which gave the Irish Church the organization it has today.

Learning, Literature and Art

Latin Learning

In the eleventh and twelfth centuries there was a remarkable revival of Latin learning in Ireland. Foreign students began to come again to Ireland and Irish students went abroad to study. Flann O'Gorman, the director of the schools of Armagh from from 1154 to 1174, studied in England and France for 21 years before he taught at Armagh. The great centres, Armagh and

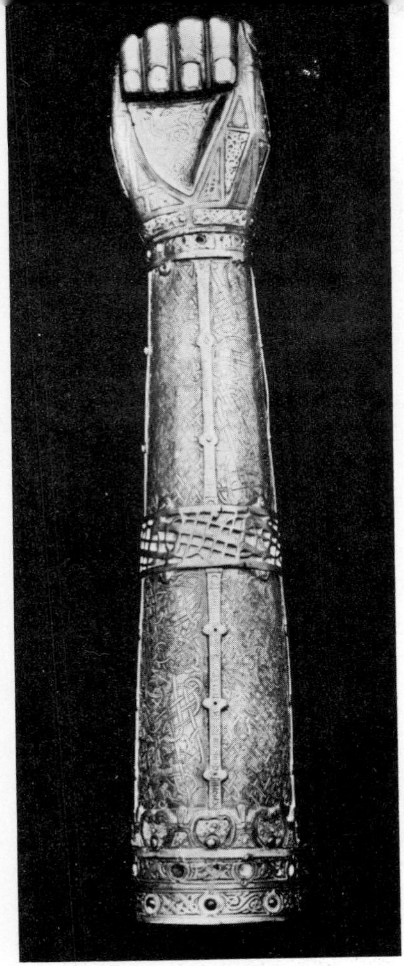

The Shrine of St Lachtin's arm, a reliquary of bronze made between 1118 and 1121 to enshrine the arm of St Lachtin of Freshford, Co. Kilkenny.

Glendalough, kept up to date in scholarship and had close contacts with the Continent. Indeed, Armagh almost became the University of Ireland. In 1162 the Synod of Clane declared that no one could teach in an Irish monastic school unless he had studied at Armagh. Rory O'Connor, the high king became its patron, and in 1169 he granted a large annual payment to maintain a professor of literature at Armagh to instruct the Irish and the Scots.

Irish Learning

An unknown number of Irish manuscripts was destroyed or lost in the course of the Viking wars. Therefore, the first duty of Irish scholars was to collect and preserve as much of Irish literature and traditional learning as they could find. They then copied all they found into large manuscript volumes. Two of the most famous of these books are *The Book of the Dun Cow* and *The Book of Leinster*.

The Book of the Dun Cow was written at Clonmacnoise, some time before 1106, by Mael Muire mac Céileachair and another scribe. It got its name from the legend that it was written on the hide of St Ciarán's dun cow. Only 67 vellum leaves of the original book survive. It contains a copy of Táin Bó Cualgne, a collection of Ulster sagas, some voyage tales and a copy of Adomnán's 'Vision of Heaven and Hell'.

The Book of Leinster was written by six different scribes, including Aed mac Crimthainn, Abbot of Terryglass. Finn O'Gorman, Bishop of Kildare, took a deep interest in the work. It was written between 1151 and 1189, though some additions were made later. It contains the legendary history of Ireland from the earliest times, lists of the kings of Ireland, long and detailed genealogies of the great ruling families, historical poems, and copies of many of the finest Irish tales including Táin Bó Cualgne.

The Writings of the Irish Scholars

The scholars of the eleventh and twelfth centuries composed new learned works about Ireland. The final version of the

Bective Abbey.

Leabhar Gabhála, 'The Book of the Conquests' was composed in the eleventh century. It contains the legendary history of Ireland and her invaders from Noah's flood to the coming of St Patrick. It is a mixture of history and story, of pagan and Christian learning, which pretends to be the early history of Ireland. Another work, the *Dindshenchas*, 'Stories of the Famous Places' was put together in the eleventh century. It is a collection of prose and verse which explains the names of the famous places of Ireland and relates the stories and legends about them. Two other famous books were written at this time: *The Book of Rights*, which describes the rights and tributes of the kings and kingdoms of Ireland, and *The Wars of the Gael and the Gall*, an account of the Viking wars and of the victories of Brian. But the scholars also wrote stories and poems, for the Irish loved a good tale. Tales and ballads of Finn and the Fianna grew popular amongst the scholars. The greatest collection of these tales is *Agallamh na Seanórach*, 'The Conversation of the Ancient Men' which was written some time about 1200. It contains over 200 stories, told by Caoilte or Oisín to St Patrick, together with many adventures and ballads. Scholars also translated and adapted many classical tales: The Destruction of Troy, The Wandering of Ulysses, The Wanderings of Aeneas and other tales.

The finely carved high cross at Drumcliffe, Co. Sligo.

Church Building and Metal Work

From about 1100 the Irish began to extend and rebuild many of their churches. Armagh, Derry, Tuam, Glendalough and many other Irish monasteries were rebuilt. The O'Briens extended and rebuilt the ancient monastery of Inis Cealtra, and many of the kings, especially the high king, Turlough O'Connor, were generous patrons of the Church. Cormac MacCarthy, a friend of St Malachy, built the most famous church, Cormac's chapel on the Rock of Cashel, which was consecrated in 1134. The foreign Orders, especially the Cistercians, also built many new churches and abbeys.

Irish metal workers still continued to produce beautiful objects, such as the croziers of Inisfallen and Lismore and the Cross of Cong which was specially made for the high king, Turlough O'Connor, to enshrine a relic of the true cross. The greater monasteries, especially Kells, Armagh and Clonmacnoise, had workshops run by families which handed down their skill from father to son. The Irish kings were generous patrons and it was they who commissioned and paid for many of the sacred vessels, crosses and shrines which adorned the Irish churches.

The handsome carved high cross at Dysert O'Dea, Co. Clare. It belongs to the middle of the twelfth century. Beneath the crucifix is the carved figure of a twelfth century Irish bishop.

Things to Do

1. Examine the map of Irish kingdoms on p. 77. To which kingdom did your locality belong and who ruled it?
2. Why was the Church in Ireland in need of reform and who reformed it? Did the Irish kings support the reform?
3. Most large libraries have photographic copies of the *Book of the Dun Cow* and the *Book of Leinster*. Ask the librarian if you may see them.

Books to Read or Consult

T. W. Moody & F. X. Martin (eds.) *The Course of Irish History* (Chapter 7), Cork 1967.

Brian Ó Cuiv (ed.) *Seven Centuries of Irish Learning*, Dublin 1961.

Ireland and the Anglo-Norman Invasion

Who Were the Normans?

The Normans were the descendants of the Viking raiders who settled in France in the ninth century and carried on successful war with the French kings. Eventually, in 911, their leader Rollo forced the king of France to make him a grant of land in the valley of the Seine. Rollo and his successors gradually added to their territory until it became one of the greatest dukedoms of France. In the course of time these Vikings became Christian, and they became French in language and customs. They were known as Normans and their dukedom was called Normandy. They were a vigorous and ambitious people who delighted in war and in the weapons of war. They were adaptive and everywhere they went they adopted the language and customs of the people they conquered.

A late medieval drawing of a Gaelicized Norman, with armour and lance. The rowel spurs which he wears belong to the late medieval period.

Medieval bowmen or archers. The Normans made good use of Welsh archers and foot soldiers in conquering Ireland. Irish people with names like Walshe, Wallace, Craddock etc. are descendants of the Welshmen who came to Ireland with the Normans.

The Conquests of the Normans

The Normans were the greatest race of conquerors in medieval Europe. They waged war against their neighbours, the powerful French dukes. There were some Normans present at the battle of Clontarf in 1014. From about 1016 they began to wage war in southern Italy and they were so successful that in 1059, by the treaty of Melfi, the Pope granted them Sicily and most of southern Italy. About this time they turned their eyes towards England, for Duke William of Normandy, later known as William the Conqueror, had a claim on the throne of England. He gathered an army of about 5000 and, with the blessing of the Pope, he sailed for England. He defeated and slew the English king at the battle of Hastings in October 1066 and on Christmas Day 1066 he was crowned king of England at Westminster. After a few troubles and rebellions, William made himself master of England, granted the greater part of the land to his own Norman lords, and established a unified and powerful kingdom. Before long, Norman lords were conquering the lowlands of Scotland. In Wales, the Normans drove back the Welsh princes and settled in the valleys and lowlands, especially in south Wales.

The Irish battle-axe and its use. Notice how the Irish wore no armour and had weapons that were a poor match for those of the Normans.

Ireland and the Normans

William Rufus (1087–1100) the son of William the Conqueror, once stood on a Welsh hilltop and looking westwards across the Irish Sea boasted that he would one day conquer Ireland. But he and his successors were too busy with their French lands and with the government of England to interfere in Ireland. Henry II, who became king in 1154 was interested in conquering Ireland. He discussed the matter with his lords at the Council of Winchester in 1155 and he sent a messenger to Rome to obtain the Pope's permission and blessing for the conquest of Ireland. However, Henry was too engrossed in his French lands and could not spare the time to invade Ireland.

Dermot Mac Murrough and the Normans

In the summer of 1166 Dermot Mac Murrough was expelled from his kingdom of Leinster and when he could find no allies at home he sailed for Bristol to seek help among the Norman lords in Wales. In Bristol he was received by Robert FitzHarding, a personal friend of Henry II, who advised him to go to Henry who was then in France. Dermot crossed over to France and after a long search he found Henry in Aquitaine. Dermot submitted to Henry II and recognized him as his lord while Henry gave Dermot permission to seek allies among the Norman lords anywhere within his kingdom. Dermot then returned to Bristol where he met Richard de Clare, better known by his nickname Strongbow, one of the most powerful lords in Wales. A bargain was struck between the two. Dermot promised Strongbow his daughter in marriage and succession to Leinster on his death and Strongbow promised to come to Ireland in the following Spring. Dermot also met Maurice FitzGerald and Robert FitzStephen, two half-Welsh and half-Norman lords. He promised them the town of Wexford and the surrounding lands, and they too promised to come to Ireland in the following Spring. Well satisfied with his success Dermot returned home and quietly awaited the arrival of his new friends.

Dermot Mac Murrough, king of Leinster (1126–1170).
Mac Murrough led a colourful career as king of Leinster.

The Coming of the Normans

Early in May 1169 about 600 Norman soldiers, led by Robert FitzStephen and Maurice de Prendergast, landed at Bannow Bay. Dermot hastened to meet them, and joining forces they marched against Wexford, which surrendered after a short siege. Dermot then turned against Ossory and the other petty kingdoms of Leinster. The high king, Rory O'Connor, alarmed at his success, marched into Leinster. Dermot submitted to him, handed over hostages and promised to send home the Normans once Leinster had been won back. But Dermot had no intention of honouring this treaty. Soon Maurice FitzGerald arrived with more forces. At last, Strongbow himself arrived with a large

The doorway of the church at Killeshin, Co. Carlow built by Dermot Mac Murrough about 1160. Though a violent and ambitious man, Dermot was a generous patron of the church.

The carved doorways of the Nun's church at Clonmacnoise, built about 1166. Dervorgilla, the wife of O'Rourke, who ran away with Dermot MacMurrough, was a generous patron of this church.

army in August 1170. He joined forces with Raymond le Gros, who had come some time before, and together they captured the city of Waterford. They were soon joined by Dermot himself and their united forces marched on Dublin. The high king, Rory O'Connor, gathered his forces to defend Dublin but his attempt failed and Dublin was taken by storm in September 1170. Dermot had now won back Leinster and hoped to make himself high king but he did not live to see the day. He died at his home in Ferns early in 1171.

Strongbow as King of Leinster

On the death of Dermot, Strongbow, according to the bargain, succeeded as king of Leinster. But he had two great difficulties to face. The Irish would not accept him and the king, Henry II, fearing that Strongbow and his followers would set up an

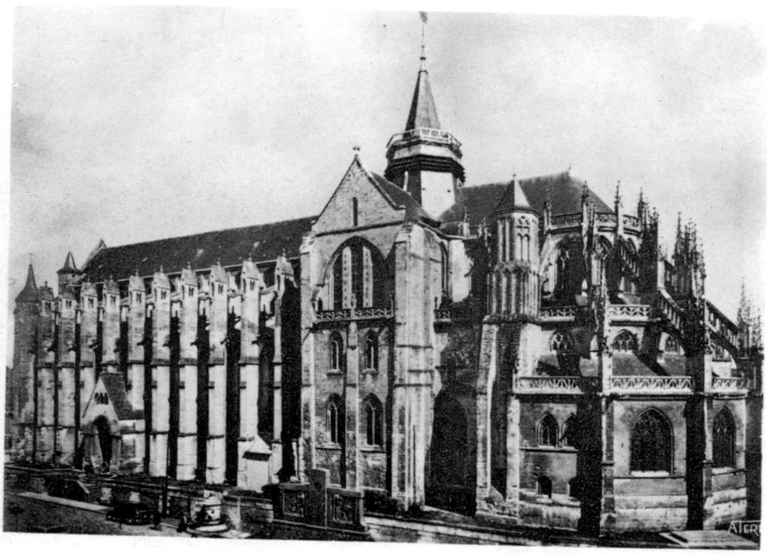

St Lawrence O'Toole, the saintly archbishop of Dublin, tried to negotiate with the Normans and prevent the fall of Dublin. While the negotiations were in progress, the Normans stormed the city. St Lawrence, the last native bishop of Dublin for many centuries, died in Eu, in France where this church is dedicated to him. His relics are enshrined behind the high altar.

independent kingdom in Ireland, ordered all the Normans in Ireland to return before Easter on pain of losing their estates in England. Strongbow sent Raymond le Gros to the king to assure him that they were still his loyal subjects and at the same time he prepared to meet the attack of the Irish. The king of Dublin, Asgall, gathered about 1,000 Vikings from the Isle of Man and the Hebrides and attacked Dublin from the sea but this attack was defeated and driven back by the Normans. The high king gathered his forces and besieged Dublin by land from July to September 1171. But just as the Normans were about to surrender they made one more desperate surprise attack on the Irish camp. It succeeded. About 1,500 of the Irish were slain and Rory O'Connor and his forces retreated in disorder.

Things to Do

1. Why did Dermot MacMurrough invite the Normans to Ireland? Find out as much as you can about Dermot.
2. Why was Strongbow in a dangerous position after the death of Dermot?

Books to Read or Consult

F. X. Martin, 'The Norman Invasion of Ireland 1169', in *The Course of Irish History* edited by T. W. Moody and F. X. Martin, Cork 1967.

Medieval archers practise their skill. Do you think you could do as well with a bow and arrow?

The Norman Conquest of Ireland, 1171—1245

Henry II in Ireland

As we saw, since 1155 Henry II was interested in conquering Ireland. In that year he received the Pope's blessing for his plan, and in the Papal Bull, *Laudabiliter*, the Pope granted him the title 'Lord of Ireland'. He now came to Ireland to make good his claim to the lordship of Ireland by bringing all the Irish kings and Church leaders to submit to him and recognize him as their lord. He feared too, that Strongbow and his Norman followers would set up in Ireland an independent kingdom in opposition to him. Expecting military opposition both from the Irish and the Normans, he gathered large and powerful forces, sailed from Milford Haven with a fleet of 250 ships and landed near Waterford in October 1171.

The Submission of the Normans and of the Irish Kings

At Waterford, Strongbow, as leader of the Normans in Ireland, submitted to Henry who then granted him all the kingdom of Leinster except for the cities of Dublin, Wexford and Waterford, which he kept for himself. Then Dermot MacCarthy, king of Desmond, came to Waterford of his own free will. He submitted to Henry, recognized him as his overlord and promised to pay tribute. Henry, in turn, recognized MacCarthy as king of Desmond. At Cashel, Dónal Mór O'Brien, king of Thomond and other Irish rulers submitted in the same way. In the course of Henry's march to Dublin and during his stay there all the Leinster rulers submitted as did O'Rourke of Brefne, O'Carroll of Oriel and MacDunleavy of Ulidia. Henry held court in Dublin during the winter, and, as their overlord, entertained the Irish kings and princes. Only the High King, Rory O'Connor, and the kings of the north refused to submit.

Why did the Irish kings submit so easily to a foreign lord? Firstly, there was no unity among the Irish rulers, and each one of them thought only of his own interests and security. Secondly, they had no loyalty to the High King, Rory O'Connor, who was a threat to their power and local independence. Indeed, they may have thought that they would be far better off under an absentee king, Henry II, ruler of England and of extensive lands in France, who would be too busy to interfere in their affairs. They were mistaken. By submitting to Henry they made him supreme landlord of Ireland and holder of all rights to land

The effigy of Henry II on his tomb at Fontevraud in France. Henry had vast lands in France and was much more French than English.

and freedom. Soon they and their people were treated as a conquered nation and their lands were granted away to Norman lords.

The Submission of the Irish Church

While Henry held court in Dublin a council of Irish bishops met at Cashel under bishop Christian of Lismore. They met at Henry's suggestion and Henry had his own representatives at the Council. The bishops passed a number of Church laws concerning marriage, baptism, the paying of tithes, and the freeing of the Church from all dues and taxes imposed by laymen. But the chief purpose of holding the council was to get the Irish bishops to submit to Henry and recognize him as lord of Ireland. The Irish bishops already knew that the Pope approved of Henry's conquest of Ireland and they probably thought that he would be a far more effective supporter of reform in the Church than the Irish kings. They swore an oath of loyalty to Henry and each bishop gave Henry an official letter of submission, recognizing him as lord of Ireland. These letters were then sent to the Pope, Alexander III, who later wrote to the Irish bishops ordering them to assist Henry in keeping possession of Ireland. The pope also wrote to the Irish kings and princes, praising them for submitting to Henry as their overlord.

The Results of Henry's Mission to Ireland

The most important result of Henry's visit was that he received the submission both of the princes and of the Church leaders. He was thus recognized as lord of Ireland by Irish and Norman, Church and laity. While he was in Dublin he made arrangements for the government of Ireland and he granted a charter of freedom to the city of Dublin. He appointed his loyal follower, Hugh de Lacy, viceroy to rule in his name and he placed garrisons in Dublin, Wexford and Waterford, Henry still distrusted Strongbow and his followers and so he strengthened de Lacy, his viceroy, by granting him the whole of the kingdom of Meath. In April 1172 Henry returned to England.

War and Conquest

After the departure of Henry, the Norman lords continued the conquest. Strongbow strengthened himself in Leinster by dividing out the richest parts of Leinster amongst his followers. Hugh de Lacy attacked the Irish kings of Meath, driving out the native rulers and settling his own followers on their lands. Everywhere the Normans went, they built fortresses to hold down the lands they had conquered. However, in 1173 there was a general revolt among the Irish. When

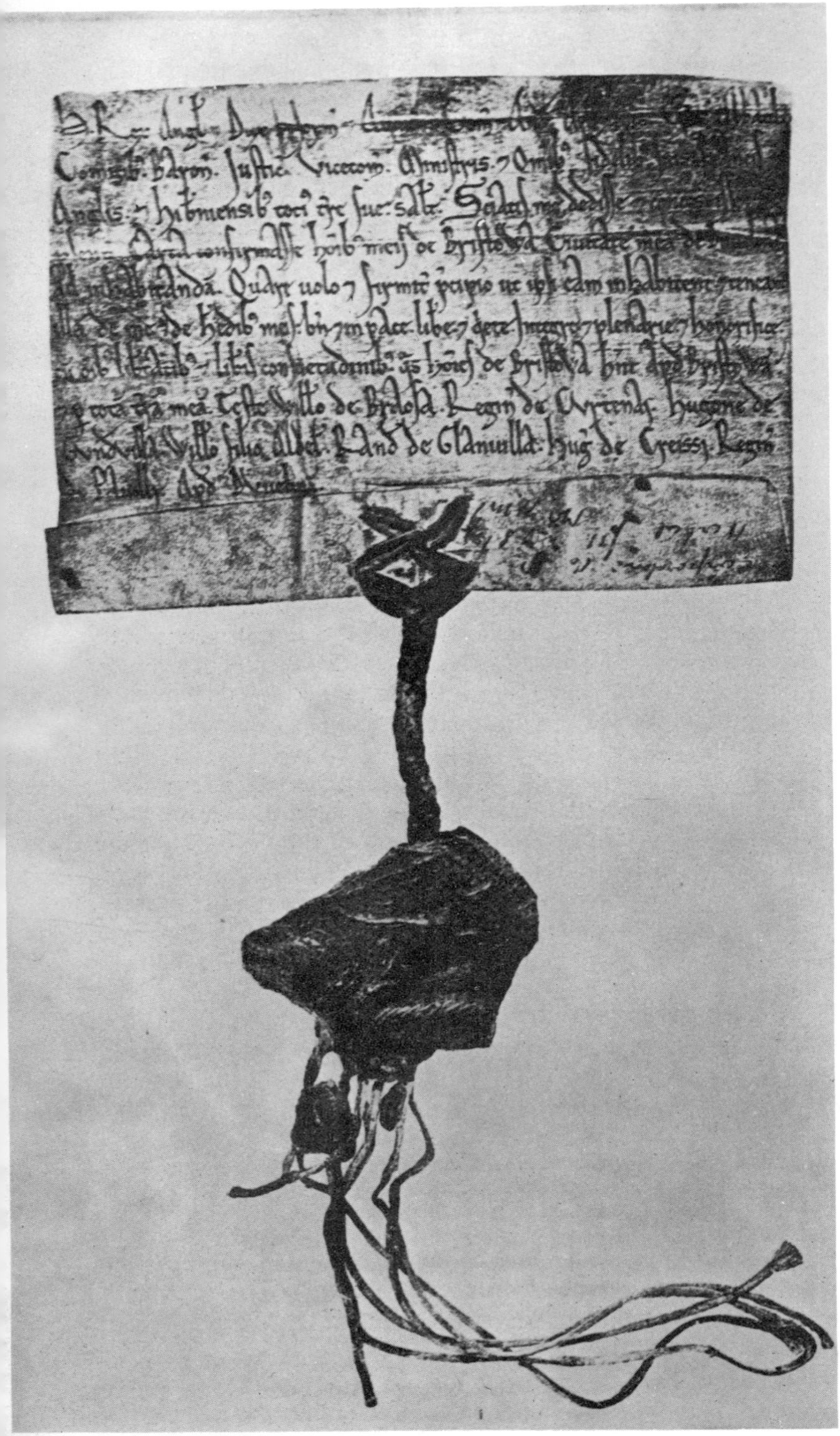

The original charter of freedom granted by Henry II to the city of Dublin.

Corcomroe Abbey, Co. Clare. It was founded about 1182 for the Cistercians by Dónal Mór O'Brien, the victor at Thurles.

Raymond le Gros attacked Munster and defeated Dermot MacCarthy, king of Desmond, Dónal O'Brien, king of Thomond, fearing that he would be the next to suffer, joined forces with O'Connor and drove the Normans out of Kilkenny. Early in 1174 Strongbow led an attack on Munster, but his army was cut to pieces by O'Brien and O'Connor at the battle of Thurles. This victory was followed by another. The High King, Rory O'Connor, gathered his forces, drove the Normans out of Meath and destroyed their fortress at Trim.

The Treaty of Windsor, 1175

Eventually, an attempt was made to bring about some settlement between the Irish kings and the Norman conquerors. After long negotiations, Rory O'Connor and Henry II came to terms at the Treaty of Windsor, 1175. By this treaty, Ireland was divided into two portions, one Norman, one Irish. Rory O'Connor was recognized as king of Connacht, subject to

Carrickfergus Castle, Co. Antrim. This great Norman keep was built early in the thirteenth century. The earliest Norman stone castles were vast fortified defences in a hostile country. The later castles are much smaller and less strongly fortified.

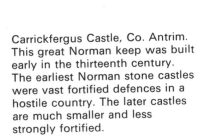

Henry as lord of Ireland and paying tribute. He was also recognized as overlord of all the Irish kings and given the duty of putting down rebellion among them and collecting the tribute due to Henry. But O'Connor was given no powers over the Normans who were subject to Henry himself. O'Connor attempted to carry out this treaty but it was soon set aside by Henry who continued to grant away the lands of the Irish kings to Norman lords.

The Grant of Munster

At the Council of Oxford, held in 1177, Henry II declared his son John lord of Ireland. At the same time, he granted the kingdom of Desmond to Robert FitzStephen and Milo de Cogan; and he granted the kingdom of Thomond to Philip de Braose. By these grants, Henry broke the treaty of Windsor and set aside the rights of MacCarthy and O'Brien, who had freely submitted to him when he visited Ireland. De Braose's attempt to conquer Thomond failed, but FitzStephen and de Cogan, aided by O'Brien, the life-long enemy of MacCarthy, were more successful. They obtained a large and rich territory about the city of Cork and MacCarthy was forced to pay tribute for the rest of his kingdom. The famous Munster Anglo-Norman families, the FitzGeralds, the Barrys and the Roches, were followers of FitzStephen and de Cogan and were granted lands by them.

De Courcy's Attack on Ulidia, 1177

The Normans now turned their arms against the north, against the kingdom of Ulidia which lay east of the Bann and Lough Neagh. The attack was made by John de Courcy, a Norman official in Dublin, who is supposed to have been granted Ulidia by the king if he could conquer it. Early in 1177 he gathered a small force and marched swiftly into the north. He took Downpatrick by surprise and he defeated the king of Ulidia, MacDunleavy and his allies in battle. Though he met severe opposition from the Irish, he succeeded in conquering all the area east of the Bann. He built castles in Downpatrick, Dromore, Newry, Coleraine and Carrickfergus, and ruled Ulidia with a firm hand for twenty-seven years. He settled his followers on the rich lowlands leaving the hill country inland to the Irish.

Prince John's Visit to Ireland

Prince John, who had been made lord of Ireland in 1177, visited his lordship in 1185. He arrived at Waterford with a force of 300 knights and over 2000 soldiers. At this time

Coins minted at Carrickfergus and Downpatrick by John de Courcy from about 1182 to 1199.

John was an ill-mannered youth who easily insulted the Irish rulers. As one eye-witness says: 'Our newcomers and Normans not only treated them with contempt and derision, but even rudely pulled them by their beards, which Irishmen wore full and long according to the custom of their country.' The greater Irish rulers stood hostile and aloof and did not submit to John. He marched through Waterford to Lismore and Ardfinnan, through Kilkenny and Kildare to Dublin, where he remained during the early winter. In December 1185 he returned to England.

By this time the most of the great leaders of the conquest—Strongbow, FitzStephen, de Cogan, Maurice FitzGerald and Raymond le Gros—were dead. The way was now open for fresh grants of land to John's favourites and followers. The Irish were weak and divided, fighting over what remained of their native kingdoms. The Norman lords in Ireland were ambitious and greedy for new lands; there was no strong hand to control them and they were often at war with their king, with one another and, needless to say, with the Irish. These were the men who now set about the conquest of what remained of Ireland.

The Normans in Munster

Already, the Normans were firmly entrenched in Desmond. Now, the greater portion of Munster was granted to them. While at Waterford John granted lands to Theobald Walter, his butler, the founder of the great Butler family. Theobald Walter was granted eastern Clare, southern Offaly, the greater portion of north Tipperary and a large part of east Limerick. Thus, by a stroke of the pen, John granted away the richest half of O'Brien's kingdom of Thomond. Theobald Walter never conquered Clare. He made Nenagh his capital and in Tipperary and the surrounding lands, he and his family, the Butlers, gradually set up the great lordship of Ormond.

William de Burgo, another of John's favourites, the ancestor of the great Anglo-Norman family, Burke, was granted a large territory in south Tipperary. He secured himself in these lands by marrying a daughter of Dónal Mór O'Brien. When O'Brien died in 1194, civil war broke out among his successors and this allowed de Burgo to strengthen his grip on his lands and build fortresses to hold down his territory. William de Burgo also received a grant of Connacht, but he failed to conquer it and his claim passed to his son, Richard. A little later the western half of Limerick was granted to the Normans and here the sons of Maurice FitzGerald received lands. In 1200 John granted the northern half of Kerry to the Normans.

The abbey of Cong, Co. Mayo, where Rory O'Connor, king of Connacht and last high-king of Ireland, was laid to rest.

Most of these lands were to fall to the FitzGeralds (the Geraldines). Thomas FitzGerald, lord of Shanid, ancestor of the Earls of Desmond, rose to great power, and he and his family gradually acquired the lands of other grantees who had died out or else preferred to live in England. In Munster, the Geraldines, the Cogans and the Barrys pressed back the Irish and gradually extended their power. After the death of Dónal MacCarthy in 1206, civil war broke out among his successors and this made their success easier. They invaded what remained of MacCarthy's kingdom and built castles all over Cork and Kerry. The Irish annalists tell us that at this time 'the foreigners overran all Munster in every direction from the Shannon to the sea'.

The Norman Attack on Ulster

John de Courcy had already conquered Ulidia, the area east of the Bann and Lough Neagh. The kingdom of Meath was held by de Lacy and thickly settled by the Normans. Between the two, and stretching north-east, lay the kingdom of Oriel ruled by O'Carroll. When Murrough O'Carroll, the last king of Oriel, died in 1189, John granted away the greater part of his kingdom to Bertram de Verdon and Roger Pipard. They expelled the Irish landowners and planted the land with their own followers and undertenants.

Now the Normans advanced against the independent kingdoms of the north-west, Tír Conaill and Tír Eogain. They were attacked from three sides. In 1212 Gilbert de Angulo (Costello) attacked from the north-west, from his castle at Caol Uisce on the Erne. From the north, by sea, came the attack of Alan FitzRoland, lord of the Scots of Galloway, who had been granted the whole coastline from Derry to the Glens of Antrim.

John, king of England and Lord of Ireland. From the illustrated charter-roll of Waterford.

Carved figures of soldiers from Roscommon Abbey which was founded by Felim O'Connor, king of Connacht, in 1253.

The viceroy attacked from the south, leading his forces northwards to Clones. But the attempt failed. Aodh O'Neill, king of Tír Eogain, and his supporters, defeated the invaders and burned the castles at Clones and Caol Uisce.

After the death of Aodh O'Neill in 1230 civil war broke out among the ruling families. This weakened the northern kingdoms so much that in 1238 the viceroy was able to invade them and take their hostages. About that time Maurice

FitzGerald was granted Tír Conaill, but his many attempts to conquer it ended in failure.

The Conquest of Connacht

Some time before he became king, John granted the whole or part of Connacht to William de Burgo, but he failed to conquer it and his claim passed to his son, Richard. Cathal Crobhderg, king of Connacht, died in 1224 and two years later his son and successor, Aodh, was summoned to Dublin to surrender his kingdom for his own and his father's disloyalty. In 1227 Richard de Burgo was granted the kingdom of Connacht except for an extensive area about Athlone which the king reserved for himself. Immediately a number of successful attacks were made on Connacht. Rivalries and wars among the ruling families of the O'Connors allowed the conquest to go ahead. Finally, in 1235 the great Norman lords of Ireland mustered their forces, invaded Connacht and conquered it for de Burgo. Felim O'Connor, king of Connacht, was allowed to hold extensive lands in Roscommon for a yearly tribute of £300. De Burgo held the remainder of the province and divided it out among the great Norman lords who had helped him conquer it. However, these men were too busy with their great estates elsewhere to bother overmuch with Connacht. De Burgo built a castle at Loughrea, made it his chief centre and settled the surrounding country with Normans. However, Connacht was never settled thickly with Normans, and de Burgo's own descendants, the MacWilliam Burkes of Clanrickard and Mayo, were among the first of the Normans to become Irish in speech and in custom.

The carved figure of a Norman knight from Jerpoint Abbey, Co. Kilkenny.

The Reason for the Success of the Normans at War

By about 1250 the Normans had conquered the greater part of Ireland and had settled even in the remotest areas. In fact, never again were they to be masters of so much of the land of Ireland. How can we account for their success against the Irish? The Normans were a great race of warriors and professional soldiers, and their methods of warfare were far in advance of those of the Irish. They had superior weapons. They used the long sword and lance, and mounted on their chargers, clad in coats of mail and iron helmets, they made cavalry attacks in proper military order. They were also accompanied by Welsh archers who used the deadly cross-bow, and well-trained Flemish foot-soldiers. The Irish had no professional soldiers. They went into battle unprotected by armour, used short swords, battle-axes, javelins and slings, and had no military tactics beyond the disorganized charge or surprise

A late medieval drawing of one of the Burkes of Connacht, showing helmet and armour, and a shield with the arms of the Burkes.

Coins issued by John as Lord of Ireland about 1198. The coins were struck by the Waterford moneyer, Davi.

attack. The Normans were experts in the art of fortification, and as soon as they conquered an area they built fortresses to hold it down. They first built a mound of earth between thirty and forty feet in height with a large flat space on top. They enclosed this space with a wooden palisade and built a wooden tower within. Around the bottom of the mound they dug a wide ditch and they enclosed a small area or courtyard at the base of the mound with a wooden palisade mounted on an earthen rampart. Here they built workshops and quarters for the soldiers. The Irish had little or no experience of military fortifications nor were they equipped to capture Norman fortresses. From about 1200 the Normans began to build great stone castles which you can still see throughout the country, and these, as far as the Irish were concerned, were practically impossible to capture.

The Irish rulers, divided and often bitterly at war with one another, struggling individually with no common plan, and equipped with outmoded weapons, could offer little resistance as the tide of Norman conquest rolled over Ireland.

Things to Do

1. Why were the Irish unable to drive out the Normans? Make a list of the reasons why the Normans were successful.
2. Find out what great Norman families lived in your part of the country and find out as much as you can about them.
3. Many people living in Ireland have Norman surnames such as Fitzgerald, Roche, Burke etc. Make as long a list as you can of Norman surnames still found in Ireland. Is your own surname Irish, Norman or English?

Life in Anglo-Norman Ireland

Feudalism

The Normans introduced a new method of government and land-holding to Ireland—feudalism which was in use all over western Europe. According to feudal law, the king was the owner of all the land of Ireland and he could grant it out to his followers as he wished. A man did homage to the king as his lord and swore an oath to be faithful to him at all times and to render certain dues and services. In return the king granted the lord a fief or territory. For example, Henry II granted the kingdom of Meath to Hugh de Lacy in return for a service of fifty knights. This meant that Hugh de Lacy was granted the kingdom of Meath as a fief but he had to provide fifty knights-at-arms when the king summoned his forces to go to war. Strongbow was granted the kingdom of Leinster as a fief in return for a service of 100 knights, and so he had to provide 100 knights for the king's army. These tenants of large fiefs who held their lands directly from the king were called tenants-in-chief.

The Division of the Fief

The tenants-in-chief could not, of course, manage their large fiefs by themselves. They kept portion of their estates as demesnes and divided out the rest among lesser lords. These lesser lords did homage to the tenants-in-chief and swore

Away from the battle, a splendidly attired medieval knight talks to the ladies fair.

Mowing hay.

an oath to be faithful to them. In return, they received a fief and were bound to supply one or many knights, depending on the size of their fiefs. Strongbow, for example, kept for himself a large territory around Wexford and an area stretching westwards towards Waterford; the remainder he divided out among his followers, Raymond le Gros, Maurice FitzGerald and others. Many of these lesser lords had sub-tenants in the same way. From early in the thirteenth century the feudal lords no longer provided knights for the king's army but they paid a money rent, called scutage, instead.

The Manor

The manor was the estate on which the subjects of the feudal lord lived and worked. In Norman Ireland it was usually identical in size with the parish. It was divided into two portions: the demesne land, usually between 500 and 750 acres, which the lord kept for himself and from which he drew his income; and the tenancies, small-holdings which the lord let to tenant farmers in return for rent and services. There were two main types of people in the manor: those who were freemen and those who were serfs bound to the land.

Two peasants make heavy work of sawing a plank.

Netting fish from a boat.

The Free Tenants

There were three main types of freemen in the manor. Firstly, there were the tenants who held lands at a fixed rent and whose lands passed from father to son. Secondly, there were farmers who held their land on lease for a number of years and tenants-at-will. These paid a money-rent for their lands and they owed the lord labour services on the demesne, usually a few days ploughing, hay-making, reaping and carting corn. Lastly, there were the cottiers who held only their cottages and a little land. They paid a rent for their cottages and did labour service for the lord as well. However, most of them were farm labourers who worked permanently on the demesne and who were paid a small wage. Who were these free tenants? In the south and east of Ireland, where there were many feudal manors, the majority of them were English and Welsh peasants who came to Ireland from the west of England, Devon and Cornwall, and from Wales. They came in great numbers, following in the wake of their feudal lords and hoping to better themselves in Ireland. In some parts, particularly in Leinster and east Munster, English settlers and their descendants formed over half the population. However, in many manors Irishmen were free tenants, particularly in the upland areas.

Serfs or Betaghs

The unfree tenants or serfs, who were called betaghs, were practically all Irishmen. They lived as family groups under

Tending pigs in the woods.

A farmer brings his corn to the mill to be ground. The lord of the manor often owned the mill and the peasant had to pay for the use of it.

their own headmen in distinct townlands. The average holding of a betagh was between 40 and 60 acres. They were bought and sold with the estate, they had no right to the land, and their goods and property were at the disposal of the lord of the manor. They had practically no rights according to the law of the state. They owed the lord heavy labour services on the demesne. Every betagh who had a plough and a ploughing team was bound to plough an acre for wheat and an acre for oats in the demesne. The betaghs were bound to spend a number of days reaping the lord's corn and they were responsible for carting it to the haggard. They made hay for the lord, saved it, and carted it into the haggard. Those who had horses carted goods for the lord and delivered his messages concerning the manor at their own expense. They also provided him with fuel and the lord could buy any of their goods at what he considered to be a fair price. In the fourteenth century this arrangement gradually died out and the betaghs became tenants paying a money-rent.

Medieval peasants ploughing with oxen. Notice the heavy plough used on Norman manors.

Fishing by net in medieval times. Rights of fishing, then as now, were very valuable.

Irish Towns and Cities

Apart from the Viking cities and a few of the larger monastic sites, such as Armagh and Clonmacnoise, Ireland had no towns and cities at the time of the Norman invasion. And so, we owe many of our most important towns to the Normans. Towns and cities were granted a charter of liberty by the king or by one of the great lords. By this charter, the people of the town or city could set up their own court of law and elect their own lord mayor or reeve; and they were granted trading privileges and the right to levy tolls. The important town of Carrickfergus, with its great Norman castle and abbey, was founded by John de Courcy. Dundalk was founded by de Verdon in the time of King John, and Drogheda, the head-quarters of the Normans in Meath, was founded by Walter de Lacy in 1194. Inland, towns grew up around the great Norman castles: Athlone, Kilkenny, Nenagh, Kildare and many

A peasant sowing the corn. While his dog drives away the crows, another crow feeds from the bag of corn on the headland.

others. In the north and west, where the Irish were strong, few towns were founded. Indeed, in the Middle Ages, Connacht had only two towns of any importance, Galway, which was founded by the de Burgos and Athenry, which was founded by the de Berminghams.

The inhabitants of the towns and cities were of very mixed blood: Viking, English, Irish, Welsh, Flemish and French. Irishmen were not excluded from the towns and in many places they made up a large portion of the population. In 1307 the citizens of Drogheda declared: 'Irishmen by custom of Irish towns, being burgesses, are as free as Englishmen'. However, as the fourteenth century wore on, the towns became more and more anti-Irish and they passed many bye-laws against 'Irish enemies.' Indeed, the citizens of Galway had the rule 'that no O or Mac strut or swagger through the streets of Galway'.

The cities and towns engaged in a lively trade in wine, foodstuffs, livestock, hides, wool, and cloth of all kinds. The towns were granted the right to hold markets and fairs to levy tolls on all goods presented for sale. New Ross, Waterford, Cork, Drogheda, Dublin, Youghal, Galway and Limerick were great centres of import and export trade. Wool, hides and grain were exported in large quantities; wine, fine clothing, metals and other goods were imported. From the beginning, the towns were always loyal to their king and they disliked both feudal lords and Irish rulers who interfered with their trade and their privileges.

Medieval ladies at their spinning and weaving. Irish textiles were an important export in the Middle Ages.

The mayors of the Irish cities, Dublin, Cork, Waterford and Limerick.

The ancient seal of the city of Dublin. In the middle ages seals were used to sign official documents where nowadays we would merely sign our names.

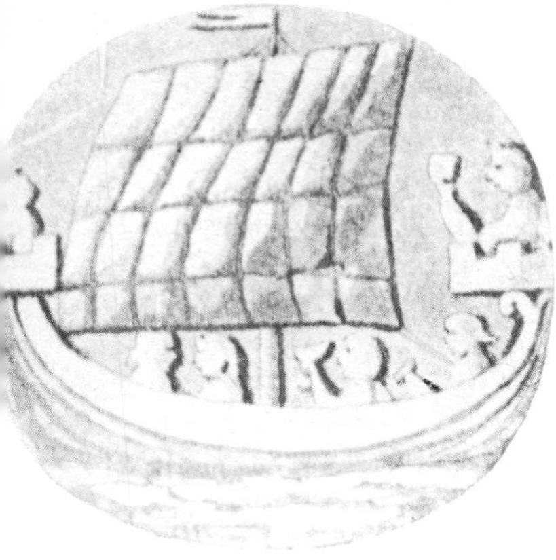

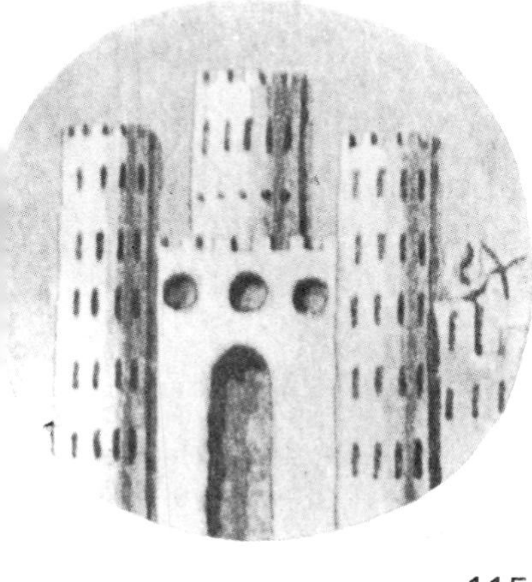

The Government of Ireland

The viceroy or deputy ruled Ireland in the name of the king. He was head of the government, military leader in war-time, and supreme judge, and he was subject only to the king himself. He swore to be faithful to the king at all times, to preserve all the king's rights and dignities and to do justice to all men according to the law. He could call out the royal army and make war on the king's enemies and on rebels. He could appoint and dismiss all except the highest of the king's officials in Ireland. He could summon parliament and pass laws. The viceroy sent regular written reports on the state of Ireland to the king, and the king sent over his officials to examine the state of the country and to deal with important business. From time to time the viceroy was summoned to England to report to the king in person. Most of the viceroys were great Anglo-Norman lords though sometimes Englishmen were sent over to govern the country.

From the beginning, the viceroy was assisted by a council, a group of important officials who looked after the everyday business of ruling the country. These officials, together with the viceroy, made up the government. Out of the council grew up the departments of state. The most important of these were the exchequer, which kept accounts of all money spent and of all taxes and income received by the government, and the chancery, which issued and kept records of all official documents.

Irish pennies minted in the reign of Henry III (1216–1272).

The Parliament

From time to time, parliaments were summoned by the viceroy to discuss the affairs of the country. Parliament was at first made up of the viceroy's council and the great feudal lords, and it met to discuss important business, and sometimes to pass laws. The first Irish parliament of which we have a record met in 1254. Later, representatives of the counties and the towns (the commons) were summoned to parliament. There were two divisions or houses of parliament: the House of Lords, made up of the great feudal lords, the bishops and the abbots of the great monasteries; and the House of Commons, the representatives of the counties and the towns.

The medieval Irish exchequer or department of finance. The board covered with squared cloth is a counting table used to calculate sums of money.

Jerpoint Abbey, Co. Kilkenny. Jerpoint, a Cistercian abbey, was founded about 1180. The cloister and tower date from the fifteenth century.

Holy Cross Abbey, Co. Tipperary founded in 1180 by Donnchadh Cairbreach O'Brien.

Culture and Learning

In its hey-day, before the Irish revival and the wars that followed, the Norman colony in Ireland was rich and prosperous. As one historian writes:

> It was a land of manors and villages, with broad fields, tilled in strips; a land of castles and small cottages, markets and fairs, parish churches, alleys and friaries. Great progress was made everywhere in the arts of peace. Forests were cleared and new land was ploughed as new methods of agriculture were introduced. Commercial life expanded and trade boomed.

The Normans were generous patrons of the Church. They founded nine new Cistercian abbeys, nine Benedictine monasteries, sixteen houses of Augustinian canons, and many houses for other religious orders. The great lords endowed these houses with large grants of land and everywhere they were centres of Norman influence. The Gothic style of architecture was introduced. Many of the Dominican and Franciscan houses and some of the cathedrals maintained schools. In 1320 the Archbishop of Dublin founded a university, but it did not succeed. However, scholars studied abroad in Paris and Montpellier, and particularly at Oxford. The Norman noblemen spoke French and were French in culture. They brought with them to Ireland the idea of chivalry and courtly love. French love songs were sung in the streets of Kilkenny and many Irish love poems and ballads go back to the new love poetry introduced by the Normans. In the towns, the various guilds of tradesmen, carpenters, tailors and so on, produced miracle plays and literature was written in French and later in English. In the fourteenth century an anonymous poet sang:

> I am of Ireland
> And of the holy land of Ireland;
> Good sir, pray I ye
> For of sainte charity
> Come and dance with me
> In Ireland.

Geoffrey de Marisco, the king's viceroy in Ireland 1215–1221. This effigy is taken from his tomb in Hospital Church, Co. Limerick.

Things to Do

1. Discover as much as you can about feudalism in England and on the continent.
2. Ask the librarian if there is a history of your city or county. He may also be able to tell you where you will find articles about your part of the country. Find out as much as you can about it and write an account of it.
3. Make a list of the benefits conferred on Ireland by the Normans. Did they do more good than harm?

4. Compare the government of Ireland in the Middle Ages with the government to-day. Is the Dáil a parliament?
5. Many abbeys and monasteries were founded by the foreign religious orders. Find out if any were founded in your locality and examine the ruins.
6. All over Ireland there are ruins of castles and fortified houses. Who built them and why were they built? Make a list of those in your own locality and examine them.

Books to Read or Consult

R. E. Oakeshott, *A Knight and his Weapons*, London 1964.
Fr Colmcille, *The Story of Mellifont,* Dublin 1958.
H. G. Leask, *Irish Castles*, Dundalk 1941.

Henry of London, archbishop of Dublin, who was Viceroy in Ireland from 1221 to 1224.

Monks singing their office. Notice the playful sketches of the demons in the corners.

Gaelic Rulers and Norman Conquerors

The Norman colonists settled on the plains, along the coasts and beside the rivers. They left the highlands, the bogs, the deep woods and the rough land to the Gaelic rulers. Indeed, they could not expel the Irish from these areas even if they wished. Many Gaelic rulers were left in possession of part of their original kingdoms and they paid tribute to the Norman lords. Each Gaelic ruler was responsible for the good conduct of his followers. De Lacy, for example, drove the native rulers, the O'Melaghlins, out of Meath and they settled in the wilder country to the west. When Strongbow divided out Leinster he granted the best lands to his own followers. However, he left Ferns and a large area north of Wexford harbour to the MacMurroughs; and the inland and mountainous areas of Wexford were left to MacMurrough's son, Dónal Kavanagh and his successors.

Other Gaelic ruling families were driven out of their native territories. The O'Tooles and O'Byrnes, who ruled the plains of Kildare were driven into the mountains of central and north Wicklow. The MacCarthys and O'Sullivans, whose ancestors once ruled Cashel, were being driven from the plains of Tipperary even before the Norman invasion. They were eventually driven into Desmond—into Cork and south Kerry—by O'Brien and the Normans. In this way, old kingdoms disappeared and new kingdoms arose. These great families came into their new lands as conquerors and won their land by the sword. In fact, they were as much conquerors as the Normans themselves. They occupied the land, drove out the older native rulers, and set up their own kingdoms. The MacCarthys drove the O'Donoghues from west Cork and took their lands. In the same way, the O'Sullivans expelled the native rulers of south Kerry. In the north, the O'Dohertys, cousins of the O'Donnells, captured Inishowen and drove out the O'Gormleys. All over Ireland, the great lords, both Norman and Irish, carved out new kingdoms with the sword.

Norman Policy

The Normans were not able to conquer the Irish completely and occupy all Ireland. Instead, they tried to control the Gaelic rulers. From among the royal heirs they chose a tame one who was willing to govern his people according to their wishes. They made good use of the frequent wars of succession

A Norman knight in armour from a carving in Kilfane church, Co. Kilkenny. This is probably Thomas Cantwell who died about 1320.

amongst the Irish and supported now one side, now the other. The Gaelic rulers made efforts to remain at peace with the Normans. They even appealed to the king to protect them against the feudal lords. When King John visited Ireland in 1210, the greater Gaelic rulers readily submitted to him. He ordered that scarlet robes be given them and he instructed the viceroy to win over the Gaelic kings. But the loyalty of the Gaelic rulers did not protect them from the greed of the Norman lords and the government in Dublin, even if it wished, could not control the Normans. The Normans had expanded very rapidly and had conquered the greater part of Ireland. However, the country was settled very thinly, the greater part of the population was still Irish and soon the Gaelic rulers began to make successful war on the colonists.

The Irish Revolt: the Battle of Down 1260

In 1258, Brian O'Neill, king of Tír Eoghain, one of the most ambitious of the Gaelic rulers, attempted to revive the old high-kingship. Aodh O'Connor and Tadhg O'Brien met O'Neill in conference at Caol Uisce on the Erne and recognized him as king of Ireland. This was the first attempt to form an Irish confederacy against the Normans, but the attempt failed. O'Neill and his supporters attacked Downpatrick in 1260 but they were heavily defeated and O'Neill himself was slain.

The Irish Revolt in the South, 1261

In 1250, John FitzThomas of Shanid, the head of the Munster Geraldines, was the most powerful lord in Munster and in 1259 he received a royal grant of all Desmond and the Decies. Desmond itself was ringed with Norman castles. Finín MacCarthy and his brothers, Cormac and Dónal, rose in rebellion and destroyed six Norman castles. John FitzThomas called on the viceroy for help. The viceroy led a feudal army into Munster where he was joined by John FitzThomas and the Normans of Munster and their united forces marched against MacCarthy. At Callann, near Kenmare, in July 1261, the two forces met and MacCarthy inflicted a crushing defeat on the Norman forces. FitzThomas himself and his son, Maurice, were slain and the old Norman power in Munster was broken forever. The MacCarthys made themselves lords of all the lands from Blarney to Dingle Bay. At this point, the MacCarthys split into two great branches: MacCarthy More, who ruled an area of 2000 square miles, stretching from Mallow to Dingle Bay; and MacCarthy Reagh, who ruled 600 square miles, stretching from Bantry Bay to Bandon. The MacCarthys remained subjects in name only to the earls of Desmond to whom they paid a rent.

A gaelicized Norman man-at-arms from a late medieval drawing in a manuscript genealogy of the Burkes of Connacht.

The Coming of the Gallowglasses

Dónal Óg O'Donnell was reared in western Scotland, where he married Caitríona, the daughter of Eoin MacSweeney. He succeeded to the kingship of Tír Conaill in 1258 and brought over with him a force of gallowglasses under the command of his father-in-law. The gallowglasses were professional soldiers from Argyle and the western isles of Scotland who fought for land and pay. Clad in helmets and coats of mail, they wielded the heavy battle axe and fought in military formation. For the next three centuries, the gallowglasses formed the backbone of the Irish forces. The MacSweeneys were granted lands by O'Donnell in reward for their services. The MacDonnells, Lords of the Isles, became O'Neill's captains and related families, the MacRorys, the MacSheehys and MacAlisters, crossed over to Ireland and took up service with Gaelic kings. Now, for the first time, the Gaelic rulers had professional soldiers on whom they could rely. O'Donnell himself made good use of his gallowglasses and when he died in 1281 he was lord of Tír Conaill, Brefne, Fermanagh and part of Connacht.

The Continuation of the Irish Revolt

From 1260 onwards, the Irish revolt against the Norman lords and against the Dublin government grew in boldness and success. It was not a united national revolt but a series of local wars carried on by individual Gaelic rulers against Norman lords. The Norman lords themselves were not united nor were they always loyal to the government in Dublin. Indeed, in 1264–5, the Geraldines captured the viceroy himself and open warfare broke out between the great Norman lords. In 1270, the O'Connors of Connacht were in revolt and Aodh O'Connor inflicted a crushing defeat on the viceroy and on Walter de Burgo. O'Connor then joined forces with O'Donnell and destroyed the Norman castles of Roscommon and Sligo; and in 1272 he ravaged the lands of the Normans of Meath.

It became more and more difficult for the viceroy and his government in Dublin to defend the Norman colony. In 1271, the viceroy had to go to war with the O'Byrnes and O'Tooles in Wicklow. They raided the lowlands and later defeated the Normans at Glenmalure. Connacht remained in a constant

A drawing of one of the Burkes of Connacht from the late medieval manuscript.

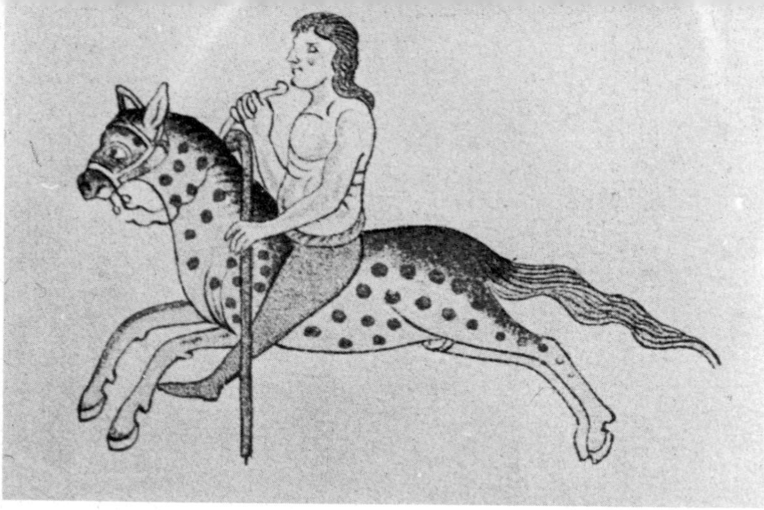

Drawings of Irish people from a medieval manuscript.

state of disturbance. In 1281 the annals tell us that 'there was great and general warfare between the Foreigners and the Gaeil.' In 1283, there was general war in Leinster; in 1289, the Irish of Meath were in rebellion and, in the same year, the viceroy had to lead his forces against the Gaelic rulers of Leix and Offaly; and in 1294, the MacMurroughs, O'Byrnes, O'Tooles and other Gaelic rulers of Leinster were in revolt. Again, from 1301 to 1310 the colony faced a massive uprising of the Irish of Leinster.

A bold attempt was made by the Norman, de Clare, to conquer all Thomond, which was granted to him in 1276. The struggle continued for many years with varying success and with Normans and Irish on both sides. Finally in 1287, Turlough O'Brien ousted de Clare. In 1318, at the battle of Dysart, the Normans were finally defeated and from that time forward the O'Briens were supreme in Thomond.

The Weakness of the Colony

The Norman conquest of Ireland was carried out by Norman lords acting for themselves with little support from the kings of England. They tended to look on their estates as lands won by themselves and defended by their own strength. Their first

A richly carved tomb in Sligo Friary. The friary was founded for the Dominicans in 1252 by Maurice Fitzgerald. It was rebuilt in 1416 after a fire.

loyalty was to themselves and their own interests. They were at war with the Gaelic rulers, with one another, and often with the king's viceroy in Ireland. In the greater part of the country, few Norman or English colonists settled and tilled the land and the bulk of the population remained Irish. At the same time, the Gaelic rulers held extensive lands, especially in the highland and wooded areas and they could attack the colony at every opportunity. All about them, the Normans had Irish tenants, servants and soldiers and their neighbours, sometimes enemies, sometimes friends, were the Gaelic rulers. In a word, the Norman conquest went too far too fast and was too thin to last.

The viceroy's government in Dublin seldom had the strength to keep firm control over the great Norman lords and Gaelic rulers. The English kings apart from Henry II and John never visited Ireland. The viceroys were frequently great Norman Irish lords who used the office to strengthen themselves. This led to violent quarrels and even to open war among the Normans. From about 1250, the English king looked on Ireland as a source of men, money and supplies for his foreign wars. The Normans of Ireland were fighting for the king's army in Scotland in 1296, in Flanders in 1297 and again in Scotland in 1301 and 1303. At the same time, large sums of money and large quantities of goods were drawn from Ireland to pay and provision the king's army in Scotland. By 1310, the viceroy's government in Dublin no longer had enough money to defend the colony. The Gaelic rulers, often openly allied with the Norman lords, went into rebellion and attacked the viceroy's forces with growing success.

The Normans formed only a small part of the population of Ireland and in order to govern their lands and do their daily business the Normans had to learn the language of the people, Irish. From the beginning they married Irish wives. The second generation of Normans spoke Irish as well as French and gradually adopted Irish habits and customs. They took part on both sides in wars among the Irish and had Irish allies in wars among themselves. As time wore on, they became more and more Irish in spirit. When, for example, the Irish of Leinster rose in rebellion in 1309, many Norman lords came out with them. By 1300, especially in the remoter areas, many of the Normans had adopted Irish dress, Irish fashions and Irish marriage customs and had begun to change over from feudal law to Irish law.

By 1315, the viceroy's government in Dublin was crippled because of lack of money; the Irish were revolting successfully in Leinster and elsewhere; and the loyalty of the Normans could no longer be relied upon. Indeed, the colony was almost on the verge of collapse. At this point, Edward Bruce, brother of Robert Bruce, king of Scotland, invaded Ireland.

Things to Do

1. Find out as much as you can about the gallowglasses, their weapons, their habits and their names.
2. What reasons were there for the decline of the Norman colony in Ireland after 1260? Why couldn't the government in Dublin defend it?

Books to Read or Consult

Eoin MacNeill, *Phases of Irish history* (Chapter 12), Dublin 1968.

The Bruce Invasion of Ireland 1315–18

Why Bruce Invaded Ireland

Until his death in 1307, king Edward I had been engaged in a long and bitter war with Scotland. His son, Edward II (1307–27) continued the war but he was largely unsuccessful and the Scottish king, Robert Bruce, won victory after victory. Finally, at the Battle of Bannockburn in 1314 the Scots won a decisive victory over the English. Now Robert Bruce was able to carry the war into Ireland.

Bruce had good reason to attack Ireland. Ireland was a source of men, money and supplies for the English king. Throughout the war against Scotland and at the Battle of Bannockburn itself, the Norman Irish lords fought on the side of the English king. As far as Robert Bruce was concerned an attack on Ireland would cut off the English king's sources of supplies, create new troubles for him in Ireland, and, if Ireland could be conquered, it would provide a kingdom for his brother, Edward Bruce. There were long connections between the Bruces and northern Ireland. Robert Bruce himself was once a refugee in Ireland and he spent the winter of 1306–7 on Rathlin Island. He was married to a daughter of the Red Earl of Ulster and he had a distant claim to lands along the north east coast of Ireland. Already, there were some Scottish settlers in Antrim and the coming and going of gallowglasses kept Ireland and Scotland in close touch with each other.

The Invasion of Edward Bruce

Plans for invading Ireland probably began after Bannockburn (1314). Robert Bruce wrote to the kings of Ireland to win them over to his side telling them 'that with God's will your nation may be able to recover her ancient liberty'. His brother, Edward Bruce, landed suddenly at Larne in May 1315 with a force of 6000 men. He easily defeated the local forces and was soon joined by O'Neill, O'Catháin, O'Hanlon and other Gaelic rulers. He then marched southwards and burned Dundalk and the surrounding countryside. The Earl of Ulster gathered his forces, both Irish and Norman and marched against Bruce. But Bruce persuaded the Irish forces to desert, the Earl of Ulster was defeated and forced to retreat into Connacht. Bruce now marched into Meath where many of the Norman Irish came over on his side. He spent Christmas at Loughsewdy and

Medieval knights and archers in the thick of battle.

early in 1316 he marched into Kildare and Offaly. The country was wasted by war and a bad harvest brought famine. The Norman forces began to rally and Bruce retreated into Ulster, where he remained for the rest of the year. He held a parliament in Ulster and in May 1316 he was crowned king of Ireland at Faughart, near Dundalk.

The Rising of the Gaelic Rulers

Soon the Gaelic rulers were in revolt. The O'Tooles, the O'Byrnes and the gaelicized Normans raided the Wicklow coast. In the north Aodh O'Donnell destroyed the Norman castle at Sligo and made himself lord of northern Connacht. Encouraged by Bruce and by the weaknesses of the Normans, Felim O'Connor defeated his rivals and made himself king of Connacht. He declared that he would banish the Normans out of Connacht forever. He was supported by O'Brien, O'Melaghlin of Meath, O'Rourke of Brefne, O'Kelly and many others. The Normans, led by one of the de Burgos, marched against him. At Athenry in August 1316 the two forces met. After a terrible battle, in which losses were heavy on both

A page from a manuscript of the annals of the Four Masters, describing the events of the year 1317.

Kl. Aois crist. 1317.

Aois crist, mile tri ched, a deich, a secht.

Donnchad ua Briain, rí Muman do marbad.

(.i. in Ruaid mac Aedha mic Eoghain) Toirrdelbach mac Aoda mic Eogain do rígad do Connachtaibh.

Roibherd a Brus do tect tar a hAlbain maille re mórsluag dochum talct a bratar Edubard a Bruis, ocus do díchur Gall a hEirinn.

Maoilir de Exeter tigherna Atha Leathain do marbad la Cathal mac Domnaill ui Concobair, ocus Domnall mac Taidg mic Domnaill Iorruis ui Concobair do marbad bleoir maille fris, ocus cethrar fer decc dia muintir imaraon fris; ar bord mic Thenaig (.i. Albain) ...

(.i. baile in mótal) Caislen Atha Cliath an Cogain do brisiud.

Maoilechlainn Carrach mac Diarmata ruaid tigherna Moige Luirg, Concobar O Concobair (.i. mac Conchobair Connaig) ocus Mathgamain O Flannacain ruaid taoisech Cloinne Cathail do marbad la Gilbert mac Goisdelb co rochaibh oile.

Madhm Cille Moire for mac Ruaidri, ocus for feraib Breifne, Mac Aeda Breifni ocus Concobar do gabail ann, da mac Neill ui Ruairc, Concobar buide Mag Tigernain taoisech Tellaig Dunchada, Mathgamain mac Tigernain, Mocol mac an Magistir, ocus secht bfichit Gall ocht do muintir mhic Ruaidri do marbad ann, ocus roile nach airmhither. (.i. Gilla Isu Ruad mac an aircinnig mac Tigernain)

Mael Ioga ruad mac Aodacain saoi erenn i mbreithemhnas decc.

Ragnall Mag Ragnaill taoisech Muintire hEolais do gabail i bfeall ocus taoisech do dénam do Seoffraig Mag Ragnaill ina ionad.

sides, the Gaelic kings were overthrown. Felim O'Connor himself was slain and the de Burgo lands in Connacht were saved. Indeed, this battle put an end forever to the power of the O'Connors in Connacht.

The Campaign of Robert and Edward Bruce 1317

About the beginning of 1317, Robert Bruce, king of Scotland, landed at Carrickfergus with a large force of professional soldiers to help his brother, Edward, in his campaign. At the head of a large army, Bruce marched southwards and appeared at Castleknock, within sight of the city of Dublin. The mayor and the citizens of Dublin prepared to defend the city. They built a new wall around the quays and burned the suburb which lay outside the walls lest it provide shelter for the attackers. But Bruce did not attempt to capture the city. Instead, the army marched southwards into Kildare and Kilkenny and westwards into Tipperary and Limerick. All along their route the Scots plundered and devastated the countryside. This together with the poor harvest brought famine and disease. The viceroy's army followed close by but it did not attack Bruce's forces. Late in the spring, Bruce learned that English reinforcements were arriving and he retreated quickly into Ulster. Robert Bruce returned to Scotland and Edward and his forces remained in Ulster.

Soon, the officials of the government in Dublin began to stir themselves. A reward of £100 was offered to anyone for 'any deed committed against Edward Bruce, a rebel, being in the land of Ireland, by which he may lose life or limb'. In the late spring of 1317, Roger Mortimer, the new viceroy, landed at Youghal with powerful forces. He dealt with Bruce's supporters in the south but he did not attempt to follow Bruce into Ulster. Instead, he tried to bring the colony to order and force the Gaelic rulers to make peace. He settled the affairs of the Normans which were in confusion after Bruce's campaigns and he made peace with the Gaelic rulers of Wicklow and with the O'Connors of Connacht. Meanwhile, the king of England, Edward II, gained the support of the Pope. All Bruce's supporters in Ireland and all friars who preached rebellion were excommunicated. Dónal O'Neill, who called himself king of Ulster and true heir of all Ireland, and a number of other Gaelic rulers appealed to the Pope, listing their complaints but the Pope gave them little support.

The Defeat and Death of Edward Bruce 1318

Ever since his retreat from Limerick, Edward Bruce remained secure in Ulster. Late in 1318, he marched southwards with

Carved figures of Irish soldiers from Roscommon Abbey.

his Scottish forces, supported by some Normans and a large force of Irish. A colonial army, hurriedly collected from the gentry and militia of Meath, Drogheda and the towns, led by John de Bermingham, marched against him. The two armies met on the hill of Faughart, near Dundalk. Bruce was defeated and two thirds of his Scots were slain. He himself was killed in battle and his head was sent to Edward II. Edward Bruce's attempt to make himself king of Ireland thus ended in failure. But the Bruces' main reason for invading Ireland was to prevent the king of England from using Ireland as a source of men, money and supplies for his war against Scotland.

In this aim the Bruce invasion was successful. Everywhere Bruce's army went, it ravaged and burned the countryside and the Norman colony in Ireland never again recovered its old strength. The Irish at first supported Bruce but so great was the harm he did that, in the end, they were glad to be rid of him. The Irish annalists wrote that Bruce was 'the common ruin of the Gaeil and the Galls of Ireland' and they said of his death that

> never was there a better deed done for the Irish than this since the beginning of the world . . . For in this Bruce's time, for three years and half, falsehood and famine and homicide filled the country, and undoubtedly men ate each other in Ireland.

Things to Do

1. Robert Bruce is one of the great romantic characters of Scottish history. Find out as much as you can about him. Why did he take an interest in Ireland?
2. What effects had Edward Bruce's invasion on Ireland?

Books to Read or Consult

G. W. Barrow, *Robert Bruce*, London 1965.

O. Armstrong, *Edward Bruce's invasion of Ireland*, London 1923.

The Decay of the Colony and the Rise of the Great Lords

The Damage Caused by Bruce

The invasion of Bruce was the greatest blow dealt against English rule in Ireland since the arrival of Strongbow. Already, even before Bruce set foot in Ireland, the colony was beginning to decline. The wars of Bruce weakened the government in Dublin and brought ruin and devastation on the lands of the Norman and English settlers. The burning of the suburbs of Dublin left the government itself without offices in which to meet. The city of Limerick was so poor that it could not afford to keep the city walls in a proper state of repair. The usual taxes and monies paid to the government in Dublin could not now be paid because the cities and towns had to repair their walls and mend the damage done by the war. Bruce and his allies ruined great stretches of land which belonged to the colonists; many towns and manors fell into decay and were soon occupied by the Gaelic families.

The Irish Attack on the Colony

As the fourteenth century wore on the tide of the Gaelic revival flowed stronger and stronger. The Gaelic rulers now went into battle wearing helmets and armour. They commanded the heavily armed gallowglasses, who were the backbone of the Irish forces. They also had light-armed professional soldiers, called bonnaght and kern, whom they quartered on their own tenants and subjects. The Gaelic rulers built castles in imitation of the Normans. O'Madden built 'a strong castle of stone and wood' and other Gaelic rulers either built castles or occupied old Norman strongholds. The Norman Irish lords also employed Irish troops, made alliances with the Irish and waged war among themselves. As the century wore on, more and more of Ireland became a land of continuous warfare.

Let us take the ten years from 1320 to 1330 as an example and see what happened. In 1320, there was an expedition against the rebellious Normans of Munster, the Burkes and the Barrys, and against the Gaelic rulers of Leinster, some of whom were in revolt. In 1323, the castle of Dunamase in Leix was burned by the Irish and the flourishing manor, full of tenants and English settlers, was laid waste. In 1324, the viceroy led an expedition against the king's enemies in the mountains of Leinster, the MacMurroughs and the O'Byrnes, and the war continued into 1325. The citizens of Ferns could

This and the following picture are medieval drawings of the Burkes of Connacht. These show the arms and dress of Gaelicized Norman lords in the later middle ages.

pay no taxes in that year because of the damages of the war. At the same time there was widespread and bitter war between the great Norman lords of Munster. In 1327, Robert Bruce descended on the coast of Ulster and many of the Gaelic rulers submitted to him, swearing to be loyal to him and to pay him tribute. In 1328, Dónal MacMurrough was chosen king of Leinster and in the following year no fewer than five of the Gaelic rulers of Leinster were in rebellion. At the same time, Brian O'Brien was ravaging the Norman lands in Tipperary.

Only direct intervention of the king of England in Ireland could save the country for the colonists. This was not to come. Instead, the king attempted to raise large forces in Ireland for his wars in Scotland, and later, in France. This weakened the colony by drawing off forces which were badly needed to defend it. The colonists in Ireland complained that the king's ministers in Ireland showed too much favour to the great lords, permitting them to oppress the poor and act almost as kings in Ireland. The constant attempts of the viceroy and his government to control the great lords and put down the rebellions of the Gaelic rulers came to nothing. In 1341, the

leading lords and men of the colony complained that one third of the land of Ireland conquered by the Normans had been recaptured by the Irish. They also complained that the king's officials in Dublin were corrupt and failed to defend the colony. And all through the century, the Gaelic rulers continued to gain ground at the expense of the Norman and English colonists.

The Gaelic Conquest of Ulster

In 1333, the Earl of Ulster was slain in treachery by his own followers at Le Ford (now Belfast). The greatest lord in Ireland fell and his lordship fell with him. The viceroy sailed immediately for Carrickfergus to avenge his death but all was lost. The Norman hold on Ulster west of the Bann was lost for the remainder of the middle ages. The O'Neills and their subject rulers expanded eastwards to Lough Neagh. The O'Neills split into two great branches; the great O'Neills, lords of Tír Eoghain and most of central Ulster; and the O'Neills of Clandeboy, who built up a great Gaelic lordship east of the Bann. Along the coast of Antrim a few Norman families remained but these became gaelicized and never again did a great Norman lord rule in Ulster.

The Loss of Connacht

When the Earl of Ulster was murdered in 1333, he left an infant daughter as heiress to his vast estates in Ulster and Connacht. By law, his estates, both in Ulster and Connacht should now fall to his daughter and to her husband. But Ulster, as we have seen, was conquered by O'Neill and other Gaelic rulers. The Earl's estates in Connacht were seized by his own cousins, Edmund Albanach and Ulick de Burgo. Edmund Albanach spent many years in Scotland after the Bruce invasion. About 1335, accompanied by his Gaelic poet and a band of gallowglasses he landed in Mayo. He married Sadhbh, the daughter of O'Maille and, after a bitter struggle, he established a firm grip on the de Burgo lands in Mayo, and founded the family of MacWilliam Burke of Mayo. At the same time his brother Ulick, seized all the de Burgo lands in Galway and made himself lord of the city of Galway. He founded the family of MacWilliam Uachtarach, later Earls of Clanrickarde. In English law, they had no title to these lands and could never look to the viceroy for support. And so the Burkes of Clanrickarde and Mayo were the first of the great Norman families to become more Irish than the Irish themselves. They set aside the name De Burgo and called themselves MacWilliam Burke; they became completely Irish in language and in customs; and they ruled their lands like Gaelic kings. After 1350, the viceroy's government in Dublin no longer had any power in Ulster or in Connacht.

The Black Death

The great epidemic of bubonic plague known as the Black Death, accompanied by other diseases, appeared in western Europe in 1347. This was the greatest plague of the middle ages and the first epidemic was followed by other severe outbreaks. The Black Death appeared in Ireland in the autumn of 1348, first at Howth and Drogheda, but it soon spread

The burning of the clothing of those who died of the Black Death in an attempt to prevent the spread of the plague. This drawing is from England but similar scenes must have taken place in Ireland.

rapidly. The plague was carried by rats and lice and it was most severe where the rat population was high—in the ports, in the towns and cities, and in the manors where corn-growing attracted the rats. By Christmas 1348 about 14,000 had died of the plague in Dublin and in Cork the greater number of the citizens died. The plague was in Kilkenny in 1349 and one of the monks of Kilkenny wrote in his book of annals:

> hardly in any house did one only die, but commonly man and wife, with their children and household, went one way, that of death. And I, Friar John Clyn . . . have written those notable facts which happened in my time in this book . . . seeing so many evils and the whole world as it were in evil plight, I, awaiting death among the dead have set them down in writing . . . if perchance any man survive, or any of the race of Adam may escape this pestilence . . .

Friar Clyn's account shows the feelings of horror and helplessness of the people and he himself as he feared, died of the plague. The plague ravaged the towns and spread into the countryside, especially in the Anglo-Norman manors, where it did frightful damage. The plague also spread into the Gaelic districts but there, where there was an open-air cattle-raising people living not in towns but in isolated farms the plague did less damage. There were further outbreaks of the plague in 1361, 1370, 1384 and 1398, especially in the lands of the colonists.

A procession of monks praying and scourging themselves as penance to God to ward off the Black Death. They believed that God sent the plague as a punishment for men's sins.

It is difficult to judge how many people died of the plague but certainly in the towns and manors of the Anglo-Normans between a third and a half of the population was wiped out. The death-rate was much lower in Gaelic Ireland and the plague did little to interfere with the rising tide of the Gaelic revival. It did great damage to the colony and wiped out large numbers of the colonists, manors were left without tenants to till the lands and the lands went waste while the population of the towns fell by as much as half.

Norman Lords and Gaelic Rulers

The great Norman lords were jealous defenders of their own rights and privileges. They waged private wars among themselves and they were frequently at war with the king's viceroy. The greatest among them were the Earl of Desmond, the Earl of Ormond and the Earl of Kildare. Maurice, who was made first Earl of Desmond in 1329, was in rebellion in 1344 and it was widely believed that he aimed to make himself king of Ireland. The constant warfare among the great Norman lords was one of the great weaknesses of the colony. The viceroy's government was too weak to control them and to govern the country properly. Many noblemen who owned estates in Ireland were absentees and did nothing to defend their estates which were seized by Gaelic rulers and Norman lords alike. The great lords took advantage of the weakness of the government and, by fair means or foul, were building up great and powerful lordships. From about 1350, Kildare, Ormond, Desmond and other lords entered into formal agreements with the Gaelic rulers. A Gaelic ruler such as O'Dempsey recognized Kildare as his overlord. O'Dempsey undertook to serve Kildare in peace and war against his enemies, English and Irish. In return, Kildare left O'Dempsey secure in the possession of his lands and defended him against his enemies when necessary. In this way, great lords built up groups of supporters and allies who fought for them in their private wars. These lords were not interested in maintaining the rights of the king in Ireland or in defending the colony but in building up their own strength and independence. The Gaelic rulers themselves had advantage to gain from coming to an understanding with the Norman lords for though they were subject in name in practice they were independent.

Attempts to Remedy the State of the Colony

From about 1350 attempts were made to protect the colony and halt the attacks of the Gaelic rulers. A great council met under the orders of the viceroy in 1351 and issued a number

Sir John Moritz, viceroy of King Edward III in 1346.

of rules. The first duty of all was to defend the colony. The lords were ordered to defend the borders of their lands against the attacks of rebels both Irish and English. If they failed to do so, all the income of their estates was to be seized by the king's officials to pay for defence. The lords were forbidden to quarter their private armies on the countryside, to make private agreements with rebels or to make alliances, by marriage or fosterage, with the king's enemies, English or Irish. Four royal officials were to be sent into each county to review the troops regularly. But all these rules had little effect.

The Gaelic rulers of Munster and particularly those of Leinster remained permanently at war with the colony, raiding the border, driving off cattle and burning fortresses. Expedition after expedition was mounted against them but with little result. In 1360, the colonists sent urgent messages to the king describing the state of Ireland. They said that they were weakened by the plague and by the failure of the great lords to defend the borders. They were impoverished by the costs and by the ravages of the continuous wars against the Irish. They declared that if help did not soon come from England the colony would be lost. Finally, they begged the king to send over a great lord as viceroy, well equipped with men and money, to protect and govern the colony. The King, Edward III, answered their appeal and appointed his own son, Lionel of Clarence, as viceroy.

Lionel of Clarence as Viceroy 1361–1366

Lionel of Clarence was a handsome youth of twenty-two and he was married to Elizabeth, the daughter of the Earl of Ulster. Lionel then had a claim to the great De Burgo lands in Ulster and Connacht which had fallen to the O'Neills and the Burkes but he never was able to enforce his claim. He was appointed viceroy of Ireland with large supplies of men and money and given the task of settling the problem of the colony for once and for all. Great preparations were made for his coming. A messenger was sent to Ireland to announce his arrival and Dublin castle was renovated. The absentees—men who owned great estates in Ireland but who preferred to draw their rents and live in England—were summoned to attend him with all their forces. Great stores of arms, war-horses and provisions were laid up and in September 1361 he sailed from Liverpool with large forces.

After a short campaign against the Gaelic rulers of Leinster, Lionel set about re-organizing the government in Ireland. He met with little success in this work. Meanwhile, the wars with the Irish continued, the plague broke out again, and Lionel had to send again and again to England for more troops.

His wars against the Irish were unsuccessful in the long run and in 1365 the king himself declared that Ireland was 'sunk in the greatest wretchedness through the poverty and feebleness of his people there because of the destruction and hostile attacks of his Irish enemies'. The task of restoring the colony was no easy one. The Gaelic rulers continued to attack it with growing success and the great Norman lords cared more for their own power and independence than for the king and his government. To add to the difficulties, bitter disputes broke out between the old Norman lords, whose families had been in Ireland for generations, and the English new-comers, who had been born in England. They referred to one another insultingly as 'English hobbes and Irish dogs'. Lionel now summoned a parliament to meet at Kilkenny to discuss means of protecting the colony.

The Statutes of Kilkenny 1366

At this parliament the statutes, known as the Statutes of Kilkenny, were laid down. The introduction to the Statutes states that

> at the conquest of the land of Ireland and long after, the English of the said land used the English language, dress and manner of riding, and they and their subjects . . . were governed by English law . . . and now many English of the said land, forsaking the English language, fashion, manner of riding, laws and customs, live and govern themselves by the manners, fashion, and language of the Irish enemies, and have made many marriages and alliances between themselves and the Irish enemies, by which the said land and its liege people, the English language, the allegiance due to our lord the king, and the English laws and put in subjection and decayed, and the Irish enemies raised up . . .

The statutes were an attempt to prevent the Norman and English colonists in Ireland from going completely Irish. They forbade the colonists to make alliance with the Irish by marriage, gossipred or fosterage. The colonists were ordered to use the English language, English names, English customs and English laws; and Irishmen, living among the colonists were bound to speak English. The colonists were forbidden to trade with the Irish and they were especially forbidden to sell them horses and armour in time of war. The colonists were also forbidden to have Irish minstrels, poets and storytellers and no Irishman was to be allowed hold a parish in the colony or be a monk in a monastery in the colony.

An attempt was made to arrange for the defence of the colony. The lords were forbidden to make private peace with the Irish or to go to war without the consent of the government;

and any lord who broke a peace made by the king's officials was liable for all the damage caused by the war. The lords were forbidden to keep private soldiers except on the borderlands. And on the borders, where there was danger of Irish attacks, the colonists were not to play hurling and ball-games but practice archery and the use of arms.

The colony was now reduced to the counties and liberties of Louth, Meath, Trim, Dublin, Kildare, Carlow, Kilkenny, Wexford, Waterford and Tipperary. This was called 'the land of peace' and even within this limit the colonists were not safe. The rest of Ireland was a land of war, a land of powerful Gaelic kings and great Norman lords over which the government had little or no control. The purpose of the Statutes of Kilkenny was to preserve and defend what remained of the colony, prevent it from going Irish and keep it English and loyal.

The Effect of the Statutes of Kilkenny

The Statutes of Kilkenny were, in fact, a total failure. The Irish language and Irish names and customs continued to spread rapidly among the colonists. The very man who succeeded Lionel as viceroy was Gerald, the third Earl of Desmond, known to the Irish as Gearóid Iarla: a man who, according to the Four Masters, 'excelled all the English and many of the Irish in knowledge of the Irish language, poetry and history' and he himself was a well-known Irish poet. In one of his poems Gerald refers to the Irish as his kinsmen and he says:

> 'I prefer being with my kinsmen
> though they intend to plunder me
> than to be chained in prison
> by the Saxon King in London'

Gerald's father also wrote verse and Gerald himself was a friend and patron of the great Gaelic poet, Gofraidh Fionn Ó Dálaigh. When the king, Richard II, came to Ireland in 1394–95, the Earl of Ormond and other Norman lords had to act as interpreter for him because so few of the leading men knew English. The laws forbidding fosterage were ineffective and the viceroy himself had his son fostered by O'Brien.

The laws providing for the defence of the colony were equally a failure. The great Norman lords continued in their old ways, having Irish allies and soldiers, and they made war and peace as they wished. The attacks of the Irish continued and at the parliament held in 1368 it was declared that 'the land was at the point to be lost if remedy and help were not immediately supplied.' It was openly admitted that the lordship of Ireland 'was for the most part destroyed and lost'. In 1370, Brian O'Brien, king of Thomond, overthrew the Normans in battle near Croom, captured Limerick and made off with large spoils. In the mountains of Leinster, the Gaelic race, led particularly by the MacMurroughs, went from strength to strength. So dangerous were the attacks of the Gaelic rulers that the government in Dublin attempted to buy them off with money. In this way the famous 'black-rents' began. In 1377, for example, it was decided in parliament by the king's government and by the leading lords and the commons of the colony, to pay Murrough O'Brien the huge sum of 100 marks to induce him not to attack the colony.

Things to Do

1. Read *The Black Death* (1969) by George Deaux. This gives a full account of the ravages of the Black Death all over Europe. Do you know of any other great plagues in history?
2. What attempts were made to halt the decay of the colony after 1350? What do you think the government could have done to preserve it?
3. Why did the Statutes of Kilkenny fail?
4. Gerald, third Earl of Desmond (Gearóid Iarla) is one of the most romantic characters of Irish history. Find out as much as you can about him.

Richard II in Ireland

A portrait of Richard II, painted by the artist, J. Randall, between 1377 and 1399.

The State of Ireland

The Statutes of Kilkenny had practically no effect and the colony continued to decline. The area under the English government in Dublin shrank year by year, its income from taxes and duties fell, and the Gaelic rulers continued their attacks. In 1377 Richard II succeeded to the throne of England. At this time, the war between England and France, known as the Hundred Years' War was in progress. Scotland was allied with France and, in England, the great lords were often in revolt against Richard. For this reason, Richard could spare little in the way of men, money and supplies to defend the colony in Ireland. The government in Dublin had not enough money either to rule properly or to defend the colony. The viceroy had little money to hire and pay troops, and it became the custom to buy off the Gaelic rulers who rose in rebellion. The great lords, Ormond, Desmond, Kildare and others had no desire to hold office as viceroy and pay for the defence of the colony out of their own pockets. In 1385, a great council of the lords and commons met in Dublin and they openly admitted that they feared that 'Irish enemies and English rebels' would conquer the whole country. They sent messengers to Richard II begging him to come to Ireland or if he could not come in person, to send some great lord to defend them. Richard II, after many delays eventually decided to come to Ireland.

Richard II Comes to Ireland 1394

In 1394, England had made a truce with France, there was peace between England and Scotland, and Richard II had put down all opposition from the great lords in England. The time was now ripe for a visit to Ireland. Richard, as he said himself, came for 'the punishment and the correction of our rebels there and to establish good government and just rule over our faithful subjects.' Richard's expedition was the greatest effort made in the middle ages to establish the authority of the English king in Ireland. Great preparations were made for his coming. Stores of provisions were laid up, huge sums of money were raised to pay the troops, and messengers were sent to Ireland to prepare for his arrival. Accompanied by many great lords, Richard sailed for Ireland in September 1394 with a force of between 8,000 and 10,000 men, the greatest English army that ever appeared in Ireland in medieval times.

The court of Richard II.

Richard's Policy and the Submissions of the Irish

Richard's policy towards Ireland was, in general a reasonable one. He wished to make Ireland a land of great lords, Gaelic and Anglo-Irish, subject to his authority. The Irish kings and underkings were to surrender all the lands they had conquered. They were to swear an oath of loyalty to the king and the king was to confirm them in their 'Irish land', the land they had always held since the conquest. The rebellious Anglo-Norman lords were to be pardoned and were, in future, to be loyal to their king. Lastly, the land east of a line from Dundalk southwards and along the Barrow to Waterford was to be made an 'English land' with English landlords. For this purpose, Art MacMurrough Kavanagh and the other Gaelic kings in Leinster were to quit Leinster for ever and win land by the sword elsewhere.

Richard's powerful army soon made itself felt in Ireland. Late in 1394 and early in 1395 Richard made successful war against MacMurrough, O'Toole, O'Nolan and other Leinster rulers. At the same time, Richard began negotiations with the leading Gaelic kings. Then, one by one, the Gaelic kings submitted to Richard. Art MacMurrough Kavanagh and his subkings submitted and swore loyalty to Richard; he promised to leave Leinster and, on the king's wages, make war on rebels against the king and win new lands for himself and his people. Brian O'Brien, king of Thomond, submitted to Richard in Dublin and he later went to Dundalk, accom-

Richard II knighting the son of the Duke of Lancaster, afterwards Henry V, King of England.

panied by his followers, and did homage. A little later, the kings of Meath, Brefne and Ulster, including the greatest of them, Niall O'Neill, king of Tír Eoghain, submitted to Richard at Dundalk and swore oaths of loyalty. Later, the MacCarthys, O'Connors, O'Kellys and other Gaelic rulers submitted in the same way. Richard knighted many of them and entertained them in Dublin. When Richard sailed for England in May 1395, Ireland appeared to be settled though it would take some time to work out the details. However, Richard's high hopes came to nothing.

Richard's Second Visit to Ireland 1399

Richard left the Earl of March, heir to the English crown, as viceroy and it was left to him to work out the settlement with the Gaelic kings. However, the kings did not trust him and war soon broke out between him and O'Neill. Art MacMurrough Kavanagh and his followers refused to leave Leinster and soon the Gaelic kings of Leinster were in open rebellion. In summer 1398, the Earl of March himself was slain in battle against the O'Byrnes at Kellistown, near Carlow. Richard had already announced that he was again coming to Ireland. He was now at peace with France and he banished his opponents from England. He raised a fresh army and, accompanied by the Earl of Gloucester and other lords, he

The arrival of ships at Waterford with provisions for Richard II's army in Ireland.

arrived at Waterford in June 1399. His army immediately marched against MacMurrough but it suffered heavy losses in the wooded country in Carlow and Wexford. MacMurrough could not be brought to battle and Richard sent the Earl of Gloucester to parley with him. But MacMurrough would no longer submit and he declared: 'I am rightful king of Ireland and it is unjust to deprive me of what is my land by conquest'. When Richard heard this, he put a price on MacMurrough's head and marched against him, swearing that he would burn him out of his woods. But Richard had no success against MacMurrough and soon he received news that his rival Henry of Lancaster had landed in England, claiming the English crown. Richard sailed from Waterford only to be defeated and deposed by Henry of Lancaster, who now became King as Henry IV.

The Results of Richard's Expeditions to Ireland

The first and most important result was that Richard, because of his absence in Ireland, lost his throne to Henry IV of the House of Lancaster. The kings of the House of Lancaster had little interest in Ireland and never again during the Middle Ages did an English king visit Ireland. Instead, England continued to be involved in a long and expensive war with France and in 1447 England herself was seriously weakened by the civil war, known as the Wars of the Roses, a struggle for the crown of England between the House of Lancaster and the House of York.

The famous meeting between Art MacMurrough Kavanagh, King of Leinster, and the Earl of Gloucester. On the left Art and his followers gallop down the glen with spears poised.

Richard's expeditions to Ireland were a total failure and really did nothing to revive the colony. Only a few towns and the east coast counties around Dublin—known as the Pale—remained loyal and English. In the report of the Irish government to the king in 1435 we read that the king's 'land of Ireland is well nigh destroyed and inhabited with his enemies and rebels, in so much that there is not left in the nether parts of the counties of Dublin, Meath, Louth and Kildare . . . out of the subjection of enemies and rebels scarcely thirty miles in length and twenty miles in breadth . . .' Even this small area was under constant attack from Gaelic Ireland and had to pay 'black rents' as a bribe to the Gaelic kings. The English population in Ireland fell away rapidly. The labourers fled from the land at war into the towns or to England. The English farmers and tradesmen would not bear the heavy duties imposed on them by the lords and when they emigrated their places were taken by Gaelic farmers.

Outside the Pale, Ireland was divided into great lordships, more or less independent of the English crown. The Gaelic rulers governed their lands according to their own laws and customs and the great Anglo-Norman lords remained practically independent. Even the greater lords, the Earls of Ormond, Desmond and Kildare became more and more Irish. These lords were almost kings in their own territories and they carried on wars among themselves, made treaties and alliances, and governed as they wished.

Things to Do

1. Why did Richard II come to Ireland and how did he treat the Irish?
2. Art MacMurrough Kavanagh is one of the romantic characters of Irish history. Find out as much as you can about him.

Life and Culture in Gaelic and Norman Ireland

Kings and Nobles

In England, kingship and estates descended directly from father to son. In Ireland it was not so, and there were many royal heirs. In order to succeed to the kingship a man had to belong to the royal *derbfine*. The *derbfine* was the four generation group: a man, his sons, his grandsons, and his great-grandsons. All of these were possible heirs to the kingship, but usually the successor was a close relative of the king. It is not surprising then that there was constant rivalry and civil war among the many royal heirs, each of them striving for the kingship. From an early time, an attempt was made to control these struggles by electing a successor to the king while the king was still living. The successor was called a *tánaiste* or *rígdomna*, in English, 'tanist'. But the struggles between the royal heirs continued. This accounts for much of the war, disorder and weakness in the Irish kingdoms.

The king was inaugurated (or, as we would say, crowned) in the open air at the traditional place for the ceremony. The O'Connors were inaugurated at Carnfree, near Tulsk; the O'Neills at Tullahoge; and the O'Donnells at the Rock of Doon, near Kilmacrenan. Each ruling house had its own traditional place of inauguration. The chief lords of the kingdom and the bishops were present at the inauguration of the king. One of the lords had the duty of proclaiming the king elected. In the case of O'Connor, his chief historian, O'Mulconry, placed the rod of office in his hand. Each of the lords received valuable presents from the new king and the poets made verses suitable for the occasion. This ceremony went back to pagan times and continued all through the Middle Ages. The last instance of it was in 1592, when the famous Red Hugh O'Donnell was inaugurated king of Tír Conaill according to the customs of his ancestors.

The stone seat at Tullahoge on which the O'Neills of Ulster were inaugurated.

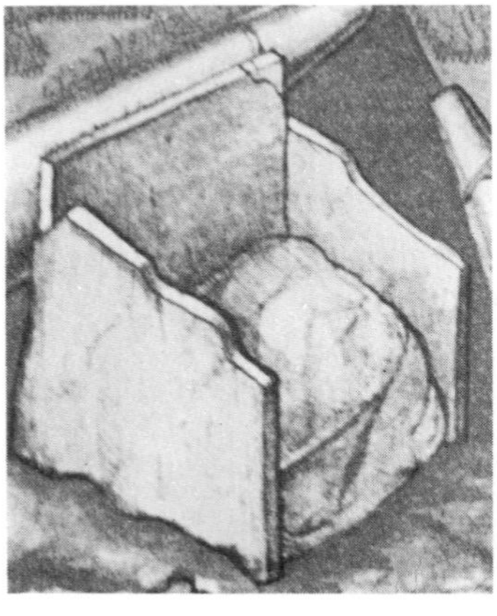

The Gaelic rulers learned many things from the Normans. Instead of going into battle dressed only in saffron skirts they now fought in coats of mail using heavy weapons. They sometimes occupied and lived in the castles they conquered from the Normans. From about 1440, instead of the massive castles which the early conquerors built, the Gaelic and Norman lords built fortified tower-houses. These were their ordinary and typical residences. They served their purposes well and provided defence against raids and forays. But the Gaelic

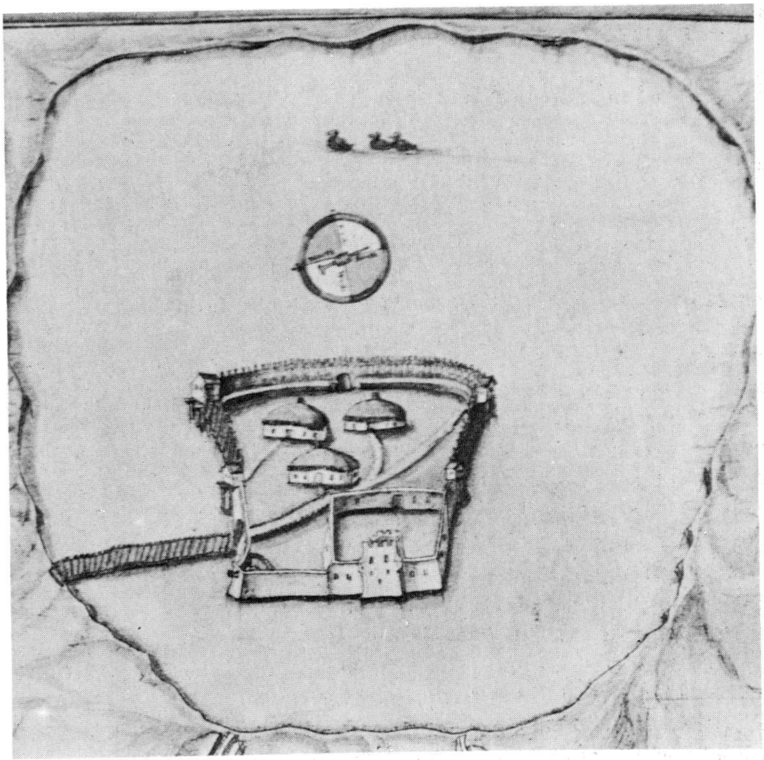

A plan of a crannóg which was still in use in 1600. Notice the shape and make of the houses.

kings, especially in Ulster and Connacht, still used *crannógs* and fortified royal *ráths* down to the time of Elizabeth. The Gaelic rulers learned the value of professional soldiers. The gallowglasses were heavily armed professional soldiers who fought for both Gaelic rulers and Norman lords. An English writer describes them as being:

grim of countenance, tall of stature, big of limb, burly of body, well and strongly timbered, chiefly feeding on beef, pork and butter.

There were also lighter troops, bonnaght and kerne, who fought with sword and shield. The same English writer describes them as 'rake-hells or the devil's black guard' because of the trouble they caused everywhere they went.

The Gaelic lords were very conscious of their nobility and high breeding. The poets reminded them of the greatness of their ancestors and the genealogists preserved their ancient pedigrees. An English writer says of them:

The Irishman stands so much upon his gentility that he terms any of the English race and planted in Ireland *bodach gallda*, that is, 'English churl' but if he be an Englishman born, then he names him *bodach sacsanach*, that, is 'Saxon churl'; so that they both are churls and he the only gentleman.

Drawings of fifteenth century Irish kings from Knockmoy, Co. Galway.

The seals of medieval Gaelic rulers. Seals were used instead of signatures on official documents.

The Dues and Renders of the Lords

The lords and gentlemen of Ireland, both Gaelic and Norman, kept private armies and ruled quite independently. The common folk under both feudal and Irish law had to pay renders and dues to the nobles. However, the nobility of Ireland mixed feudal and Irish law and drew the greatest possible income from their tenants. There was an Irish custom called *coinmed* by which the tenant was bound to provide free quarters to the lord and a number of his followers for a limited period. This custom was now extended without limit by both Gaelic and Norman lords; troops were quartered on the tenants and the tenant had to provide food and pay for the soldiers and their horses. This was known as *coign and livery*. The lords demanded an annual payment in money called 'srah' and an annual payment in cattle called 'mart'. The great lords travelled about with their wives, families and retinue to monasteries and gentlemen's houses, taking food and drink without payment and quartering their horses and horseboys on the neighbouring farmers. The lords had another custom called 'cuddie' by which the tenant had to provide them and their company with food and drink for four nights four times a year. The English tenants would not bear these taxes and payments; they emigrated and their places were taken by Irish tenants who were prepared to pay the lords their demands. These customs spread into the Pale itself. In 1410 the imposition of coign and livery was declared to be treason. A little later the viceroy himself, because

A carving of a noblewoman from Gowran Abbey, Co. Kilkenny. The carving probably dates from the fifteenth century. At Gowran, the first and third earls of Ormond are buried.

of lack of money, was forced to impose coign and livery on the farmers of the Pale. An official document of 1533 states that 'the Englishry have admitted to be their tenants those of the Irishry who can live hardily without bread or other good food; and some for greed, to have of them more rent . . .' Indeed, under the rule of the great lords, the life of the peasant was a hard one.

Brehon Law and March Law

The brehon laws were the ancient laws of Ireland, preserved and studied by a professional body of lawyers called brehons. The brehons had schools of law in which the ancient texts of the laws were studied and copied. The most famous schools were those of the MacEgans and the school of the O'Davorens in the Burren, Co. Clare. But the brehons were more than mere scholars who studied ancient texts. They gave judgement in legal cases brought before them. Varying scales of compensation were paid for all offences, even for murder—and the brehon received part of the compensation as payment for his services.

Out of a mixture of feudal law and brehon law the great lords produced the customs known as 'march law'. The Statutes of Kilkenny (1366) and later statutes forbade the use of march law but the government in Dublin was not strong enough to enforce its own statutes. The English law-courts of the Pale were themselves corrupt and even the lords of the Pale, who were supposed to be loyal men, forbade their tenants to go to them. Outside the Pale, the country was governed by march law and brehon law and, more often, by the law that 'might is right'.

The Poets

After the twelfth century, the lay poets became the chief preservers of traditional learning. Most of the great poetic families and learned men came originally from the midlands. Poetry was a craft handed down from father to son: a poet had to be 'the son and grandson of a poet'. Among the great poetic families we find the names Ó Dálaigh, Ó hEósa, Ó Cléirigh, Ó hUiginn, Mac Craith, Mac a' Bhaird and many others. The young poet spent seven years studying in a school of poetry. The term lasted from November to May. In the school, he studied the grammar of the Irish language, the art of writing poetry and the traditional learning, tales and sagas. When his studies were completed he was a professor of poetry, skilled in the use of difficult language and metres, honoured by society and richly rewarded by the nobility.

The poet composed his verses while lying on a couch in a dark room. The poem was usually a praise-poem in honour of some great king or lord. Then, in the presence of the king and his followers, the poem was recited by the poet's *reacaire* or professional reciter who was accompanied on the harp. The poem praised the king for his generosity and bravery and for his courage in battle, listed his great ancestors and urged him to imitate their deeds. For this the poet was very handsomely rewarded and given valuable presents. But the poets also wrote satires on kings and lords and their satires were greatly feared for a poet's satire was as terrible as the Church's excommunication. A satire ruined a king's reputation and men believed that the poets had the power to rhyme a man to death. Each lord had his poets and many nobles kept a *duanaire* or poem-book in which the praise-poems were written and preserved as a proud family record. The poets travelled from one great house to another and were welcome guests who were always well treated. In 1351 William O'Kelly, who had just won a large portion of his kingdom of Uí Maine, celebrated the event by giving a great Christmas feast for all the poets, men of learning and musicians of Ireland. It was a great feast, too, according to the account which one famous poet left us.

The Normans lived in a country where everyone spoke Irish and they themselves married Irish wives. They learned Irish well and they learned it quickly, as the verse says:

> Their chiefest books
> were women's looks
> which right good Irish taught them.

A fresco of a hunting-scene from Holy Cross abbey Co. Tipperary. It dates from the fifteenth century.

Cahirmacnaughten stone fort, Co. Clare. It was inhabited until the seventeenth century. Here the O'Davorens had their famous school of Irish law.

They soon grew as fond of Gaelic poetry as the Irish kings and they became patrons of the poets. As early as 1213, an Irish poet, fleeing from the anger of O'Donnell, found refuge in the house of Richard de Burgo. Gerald, the third Earl of Desmond and his brother, Maurice, were patrons of the poets and Gerald himself, as we saw, was a composer of poetry. The poets were willing to praise Gaelic and Norman patrons alike. Gofraidh Fionn Ó Dálaigh was poet to the Earl of Desmond and to MacCarthy. It was he who wrote the famous lines:

In the Galls' poems we promise
to drive the Gaeil from Éire;
The rout of the Galls overseas
In verse we promise to the Gaeil.

The English government in Dublin feared and distrusted the poets and minstrels. The Statutes of Kilkenny forbade the English to receive them into their homes. In 1414, the viceroy plundered the lands of the poetic family, Ó hUiginn. Niall Ó hUiginn satirized him and he died five weeks later, berhymed to death according to the poets. In 1430 the government forbade the English to entertain or to let land in the marches 'to Irish rhymers and others, outlaws and felons'. Down to the reconquest of Ireland in the time of Elizabeth the poets were hated by the English government. There was good reason for

The figure of a harper from the shrine known as *Fiacal Phádraig* which was made between 1100 and 1376.

doimthechtai partolin ⁊ imthechta ne
mid do innisi dun colec. Nemid am
Cuic gabala sin rongabsat heriu cos
in rea. ni ragbad ria ndile ⁊ ni ra
gbad iar ndile co torchair dibsi
ar ndile fa ri iar noul na dilend din
tir. Is ia nuim rogab mc agnomain
mc starai cos ruaib ach hel. tolo
tar for longais eschedra landana
fichet ar in marannainge caich
dib fri araile. Tre bliadna hsuind cob
ui mile mac lamo. do ernic dun eba
lin ro atomnach connd aptha tar
acht oen fer i annig nat. dig ail noho
ngaib ein eter olu nenn do innisi scel
da nanise irmsiu in fsin. Batar a
raim odangin to angin ⁊ o aill
to aill ocomoitin ar conaib altaib.
Dibsa ar nuiecat rombui heriu hi
fas. Doluid cne forin asrinnach
⁊ ado no imthect robaitea taib for
thribsi ⁊ nobitis huama aurdal
ta lim. Rogab mc agnomin iar
bratain athar dam ria ttac tin
nsor i ahallaib ⁊ baru fan i gabail
orme mongach ingnech en nocht
enos imnsoac. Baru a doci nand
incotlud conacca lorsa hinnict
huis falla ao bau u hirsuidni iarul
barru hoc maith momsin ma lim ⁊ b
arra hunnce alma so incellind.
heriund ⁊ ala mor in horraib ind
Dorrum alt conmanrsin frihan
sir nsinso ⁊ fahamsir agabala dia
elaind. Aintan toluith nsin id
tochum hsin escheopa bar ca ar

bairc immurpala muir bliadain
⁊ lech robaitea ⁊ arbaatar gorta
acht eschedra lanana immslicht for
orbairt asilsin for herind conrob
atar eschedra mili cethri lan
amna and immsliucht conroibtatt
uli huile kattre. Doluid cne fors
ra asrinnach ⁊ barru forstechud ina
ndoinib ⁊ conaib altaib. Barru ai
oci and intor huase cuimsin lim
⁊ no fstar dul assa niact in naill. lot
ru indeilb tuirc allaid sin lim on
da ⁊ maith lim momsin ma ⁊ barru
hurrice toctaib tone nerri. ⁊ ro hi
michellind heriund ⁊ nobui dunar
lim beos dachigid nsi cenichrea
hulad i nam sin moc ne ⁊ mothno
se aniss noen magin nom eloe clad
na delbaid huili togner. Na iroib
Gabair semion mc stamai i nin sid
fin tonand ⁊ fin bolg tneb sat soe
herind. Doluid cne formra ⁊ bad
inrsech inuimma ⁊ bansimoir co
acht echt natone inathse act ba
rru inhuamaib ⁊ i nallaib moc
ur lochra to morun to cumai
lim in raba noclinz moc sidan
esin biad nibui cumac. lochsa fo
eilb muin fsich main maith
on lim da basotisin momma ba
rraith sch imtoltana nolund
dar heriund nohinnaind eanet
Gabair beothecht mc iordanin.
innid sid forsnacheilu batar
and ⁊ iroib i ngalun ⁊ tuctha
dea ⁊ and se esin ela cornaf bun
ad lan nofr neplach act barric

A slate used for writing on in a medieval Irish school. It was found at Smarmore, Co. Louth and dates from about the fifteenth century.

this. The poets were the bearers and preservers of Irish culture and were a powerful anti-English force in Ireland; and they were the supporters of those great lords, Gaelic and Norman, who opposed the power of the Crown in Ireland. The Englishman, Thomas Smyth wrote bitterly of the poets in 1561:

> . . . these people be very hurtful to the common weal, for they chiefly maintain the rebels; and further, they do cause them that would be true to be rebellious, thieves, extortioners, murderers, raveners, yea and worse if it were possible.

The Great Books

In the fourteenth and fifteenth centuries, when the Gaelic revival was in full swing, there was also a revival of Gaelic learning. The traditional lore of Ireland was gathered from old manuscripts by our native scholars and written into great manuscript books. The *Book of Ballymote* is one of these books. It was written under the patronage of MacDonagh, the Gaelic ruler of Corann whose seat was at Ballymote, Co. Sligo. The book was written sometime between 1384 and 1406 by a number of scribes, including one of the O'Duignans, a famous learned family. The *Book of Uí Maine* was written about 1394 by two scribes, Adam Ó Cuisín and Faolán Mac a' Gabhann, for Muircheartach O'Kelly, bishop of Clonfert and later archbishop of Tuam. *The Book of Lecan* was compiled by Giolla Íosa Mór Mac Fir Bhisigh, hereditary poet and historian to O'Dowd, who ruled large territories in Sligo and

A page from the valuable Irish manuscript, handed over as a ransom for Sir Edmund Butler in 1462. The manuscript is now preserved in the Bodleian library at Oxford.

O'Neill's castle at Dungannon. Note the small round houses within the enclosure. You will notice that they are thatched and without chimneys, as most houses in Ireland and England were at this time.

Mayo. Each of these great books is a library of Gaelic learning. They contain the genealogies of all the great Gaelic families; lists of the kings; historical poems and tracts; religious writings and stories of the saints; copies of the *Leabhar Gabhála*, the *Dindshenchas*, the *Book of Rights*, the *Banshenchas* (a list of the famous women of Ireland) and other ancient texts. In these books the ancient learning of Ireland is preserved but at the same time new literature was being written and books were translated from other languages.

The New Literature

Much of the new literature of the fourteenth and fifteenth centuries was written for intelligent and cultured nobles, both Gaelic and Norman. Many of them were great lovers of literature and some of them, like Gearóid Iarla, were themselves poets and writers. The lords were great lovers of books and generous patrons to men of letters.

In 1500, the Earl of Kildare paid about £1500 in our money for an Irish manuscript. When Sir Edmund Butler was captured in 1462 by the Earl of Desmond, a famous Irish manuscript was given in ransom for him. The Gaelic lords set a high price on books and the Book of Ballymote was reckoned to be worth seven score milch cows, well over £7000 in our money. In his library the Earl of Kildare had 21 Latin books, 11 in French,

7 in English and 20 in Irish. Amongst his Irish books were a book of genealogies, some lives of the saints and tales like 'The Children of Lir', 'The Boyhood Deeds of Cú Chulainn' and other stories.

A great deal of the new literature was religious. The Franciscans came to Ireland about 1230 and spread rapidly. By 1350 they and the Dominicans had turned over to Irish. They brought with them books of *exempla*, stories used by preachers in sermons (and still used) to bring home the point to their hearers. These stories and tales soon passed into Irish. The *Dialogue of Christ's Passion* was translated into Irish before 1400. In 1461, Thomas Ó Bruacháin, canon of Killala, translated another favourite book, *Meditations on Christ's Life* from Latin to Irish. Various works of theology such as Pope Innocent III's *Contempt of the World* and the *Mirror of the Sinner* were translated from Latin; so also were books on confession, on the sacraments, on the death of Christ and on the martyrdoms of the saints.

Because of pilgrimages and journeys abroad there was a new interest in travel-books. *The Travels of Sir John Mandeville*, a doctor from Liège who was a real teller of tall tales, was translated in 1475 by an Irish nobleman, Fineen O'Mahoney.

In war-time cattle-raiding was common. Here you see gallowglasses marching into the fight, led by a piper; a house being set ablaze on the right; and, in the background, cattle being driven off.

The Book of Marco Polo, the Venetian who travelled as far as China, was also turned into Irish. The romantic tales of King Arthur and his noble knights found their way into Irish and tales of chivalry and bravery—of Charlemagne, of Fierabras, of Sir Guy of Warwick—were translated. Some original prose works were written in Irish. The most famous of these is *The Triumph of Turlough* which tells how the great Turlough O'Brien drove the Normans out of Thomond.

The poets wrote hundreds of poems in praise of the great Gaelic and Norman lords and many of these poems are still preserved. We still have the poem-books of the Roches, the Butlers, the O'Neills and many others. The poets also wrote a great deal of religious verse and some very fine love poetry.

Education

Education in medieval Ireland was the privilege of the few. In the colony, the local clergy maintained schools attached to the abbeys and churches. We do not know how much of the old tradition of learning survived in the monasteries of Gaelic Ireland. In Gaelic Ireland the professional poets and brehons maintained schools of poetry and law. The schools of poetry gave their students an excellent training in the Irish language and lore and we still have some of their text-books and grammars.

Various attempts were made to set up a university in Ireland. In 1338, the scholars and clerics of Ireland petitioned the king for a university in Dublin where they could study theology, canon law and civil law. Though the king approved, this attempt came to nothing. In 1465, the Irish parliament passed an act by which a university was to be established in Drogheda which could give degrees like the universities of Oxford and Cambridge. This attempt also failed. As a result, Irishmen studied abroad at Oxford and Cambridge and they studied law at the Inns of Court in London. Irish students at Oxford misconducted themselves and gave a great deal of trouble. An act of parliament of 1413 forbade them to have a separate hostel and allowed them to go to university only with the viceroy's permission. However, Irish students remained very numerous at Oxford. They also studied on the continent, particularly students of medicine, who attended the universities of Paris and Montpellier. Ireland did not have her own university until 1591 when Queen Elizabeth founded Trinity College.

The Lives of the Common People

We really know very little about the common people and peasants of Ireland during the middle ages. The peasants lived

Methers, Irish wooden drinking vessels which were used in this country from 1000 to 1600 A.D. Methers were passed round the company and people drank out of the corners.

in little hamlets or groups of houses. The hamlet had no church or inn like the English villages; it was simply a group of houses clustered together. Stone was seldom used as building material for houses. They were usually made of timber, clay, sods, or the boughs of trees. The houses of the poor and even many of the houses of the rich had no chimneys. The hearth stood in the middle of the house and the smoke from the fire escaped through a hole in the roof. The use of turf as fuel was known from the earliest times but wood was the usual fuel until the cutting down of the woods in the sixteenth and seventeenth centuries.

An Irish soldier with his horse and horseboy. Notice his dress, his tall conical cap and his great cloak. His horse has a saddle and he himself wears rowel-spurs.

The land about the hamlet was known as the infield. It was divided in strips and cultivated by the different families of the hamlet; and the strips were carefully fenced off from each other. From time to time, sometimes from year to year, the strips were re-divided among the families. When the English troops came into the midlands in 1600, they were amazed to see how orderly the fields were fenced, the hamlets inhabited, and every highway and path so well kept. Naturally, the hamlets, houses and cultivation differed from place to place. In general, agriculture was fairly primitive. The heavy plough was known to the Irish long before the Norman invasion but they generally used the light plough drawn by the horse's tail. Ploughing with oxen was known from early times but it seems to have died out in the late Middle Ages. The chief grain-crop was oats but barley and wheat were also sown. Because of the dampness of the climate, corn had to be artificially dried and hardened in corn-drying kilns. A great deal of flax was grown. This was worked up into yarn and exported in large quantities. The saving of hay was unknown in Ireland until the coming of the Normans and it was they who introduced hay-making. Even in the sixteenth century, hay-making was scarcely practised in the Gaelic lands.

Irish men at arms. Notice the sword, the short dagger and the long-handled battle-axe.

The riches of the Irish farmer lay then, as now, in cattle. 'Their plenty of grass', says an Elizabethan writer, 'makes the Irish have infinite multitudes of cattle'. The cattle were grazed in the rough land or moor around the hamlet. This moorland, mountain and rough pasture was known as the outland. Though it was portioned out among the families of the hamlet, it was not fenced or divided into lots. The people practised booleying. In the summer, after the crops had been sown, the people moved out of the hamlet into the hills and the moorland. Here they built small cabins of sods and stones and roofed them with heather. Sometimes the huts were made of stone and they were grouped close by one another near a stream or running water. The English poet Spenser wrote of this custom in 1595: 'There is one use among them, to keep their cattle and to live themselves the most part of the year in boolies, pasturing upon the mountain and waste wild places'. In the summer, the people lived upon the produce of the cows—milk, cream, and especially curdled sour milk. Sometimes they drew blood from the cows, flavoured it with sorrel leaves and used it as food. Apparently, the summer in the boolie was a happy and mirthful time. Tending the herds, milking and butter-making were the only duties. The spring sowing had been done, the harvest had not yet come, and there was time for song and merriment and courting. These customs of farming

and booleying were common in many parts of Europe and they survived in Ireland until the eighteenth century and, in parts, until the famine.

Food and Drink

A great deal of oaten and barley bread was eaten, especially thin oatcakes. Often the corn was not threshed and dried in the kiln. The woman took a handful of corn, holding it by the stalks, and set fire to the ears. She beat out the corn with a stick as soon as the chaff was burnt, ground the corn on a hand-mill or quern, and made bread of it immediately. The bread was usually baked on flagstone griddles. This bread was eaten with great quantities of butter. Fynes Moryson, an English traveller in Ireland about 1600, states that the Irish 'swallow lumps of butter mixed with oatmeal and love no food more than sour milk curdled.' The Irish also made soft cheeses from cows' and sheep's milk. In the autumn, surplus animals were slaughtered and salted down; and beef and pork were favourite winter foods. The English writer, Stanihurst says: 'No meat they fancy so much as pork and the fatter the better.' One of Shane O'Neill's household demanded of his fellow whether beef was better than pork; 'that', said the other, 'is as intricate a question as to ask whether thou art better than O'Neill'. According to a very old Irish custom, when a beast was slain certain parts of it were given to various tradesmen and members of the household:

A medieval woman's gown of woollen homespun. It was found in a bog at Shinrone and is preserved in the National Museum.

The head, tongue and feet to the smith. Neck to the butcher. Two small ribs, that go with the hind-quarters, to the tailor. Kidneys to the physician. Marrowbones to the strong man. Udder to the harper. Liver to the carpenter. A piece to the stableman. Next bone, from the knee to the shoulder, to the horseboy. The heart to the cowherd. Next piece to the housewife of the house. The third choice to the nurse. Tallow for candles. Hide for wine and whiskey. Black puddings for the ploughman. Sweetbreads for her who is with child.

The Irish drank great quantities of home-brewed beer. Indeed, a very early law-tract lays down that the strong farmer must have a number of vats of malting barley in his house. Strangely enough, there is no mention of whiskey until quite late, and then it is an unfortunate one. The first reference to it in the annals occurs under the year 1405, when Richard MacRannal, lord of Muintir Eolais, died at Christmas from a surfeit of whiskey. Whiskey must have been a common drink in the fifteenth century and the Irish flavoured it with nutmeg, cinnamon, and other spices. Wine was imported by the upper classes and there was a lively trade in wine between the south coast towns and Gascony.

Clothes

Naturally, the dress of the people varied according to wealth, rank and taste. Here is Camden's description of the dress of the well-to-do Irishmen: 'They wear large linen tunics, with wide sleeves hanging down to their knees, which they generally dye with saffron; short woolly jerkins; very plain and close-fitting trews; and over these they cast their mantles or shaggy rugs, fringed and elegantly variegated . . .' The Englishman, Derricke, wrote of the dress of the Irish kerne:

> Their shirts be very strange
> Not reaching past the thigh,
> With pleats on pleats they pleated are
> As thick as pleats may lie;
> Whose sleeves hang trailing down
> Almost unto the shoe
> And with a mantle commonly
> The Irish kerne do go.

Irish dress in the end of the fifteenth century and in the sixteenth century.

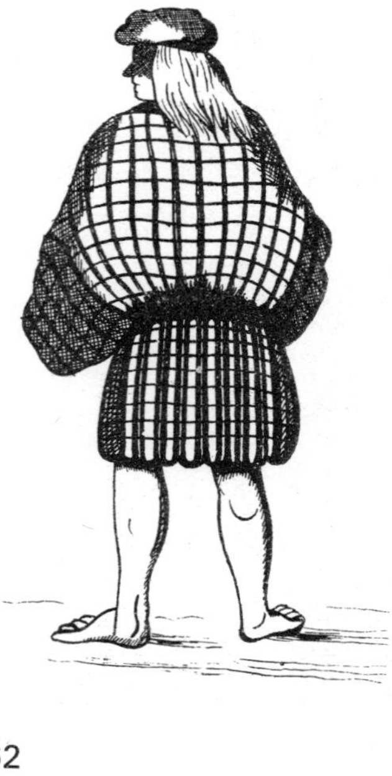

The great mantle of the Irishmen was famous. Spenser says that it was 'their house, their tent, their couch, their target. In summer, they could wear it loose; in winter, wrap it close'. Men wore their hair in long locks and glibs and had flowing moustaches. The women wore long brightly-coloured skirts, embroidered with silk and many ornaments, and tucked up at the bottom. On their heads they wore a folded hood made of linen. As usual, the dress of the poor was simpler; many of them went bare-headed, covered only by the great Irish mantle.

Festivals and Amusements

Spread throughout the year was a number of great festivals which the common people celebrated and enjoyed. Most of these were older than Christianity and were associated with superstitions and pagan beliefs. There were celebrations on May Day and on St Bridget's Day but the greatest popular festival was Lughnasa, August 1, which was considered the right day to begin the harvest and enjoy the first fruits of the new crop. The people celebrated it throughout Ireland in various ways and under various names: by assembling on hill-tops, going on pilgrimage to places such as Croagh Patrick, gathering beside holy wells and holding pattern fairs. It was a time of mirth and joy for the ordinary people especially for the young people; a time given to sports, courting and faction-fighting. The people played games of ball, particularly

A gaelicized Norman gentleman, one of the Burkes of Connacht.

hurling which was a favourite and dangerous sport. Football was played only in Fingal. They also played games of rounders and casting weights. Gambling of various kinds was a favourite pastime and there were many professional gamblers. The people had their own popular folk-songs and listened to the tales of their local seanchaí. Dancing was introduced by the Normans and it became very popular. Wakes provided another occasion for playing games and the custom of having games at wakes is a very old one found in many countries. However, the lot of the ordinary peasant was a hard one. He was looked down upon by the great nobles and by their admirers, the poets, who mention the peasant only to sneer at him. The peasant paid heavy rents and duties to his lord, whether his lord was Gaelic or Norman. It was he who footed the bill for the high living of the great nobles; maintained the clergy and the poets with his labours; and had the gallowglasses, kerne, and idle swordsmen quartered on him. The victories of Gaels or Normans mattered little to him: the one was as bad a landlord as the other.

Things to Do

1. What kind of landlords were the Gaelic rulers and Anglo-Norman lords? How did they treat the peasants?
2. Describe the training and the work of the Irish poets. Make a list of the chief poetic families.
3. Was the life of the common man in the Middle Ages a hard one? Write an account of the times of the ordinary people.

Books to Read or Consult

Robin Flower, *The Irish Tradition*, Oxford 1947.
David Greene, *The Irish Language,* Dublin 1948.
E. Knott, *Irish Classical Poetry*, Dublin 1957.
E. Estyn Evans, *Irish Folk Ways*, London 1957.
Donal O'Sullivan, *Irish Folk Music and Song,* Dublin 1952.

A Dutch drawing of the 'wild Irish'. The figure on the right is wearing the great Irish mantle.

Ireland Under the Great Earls

After the failure of Richard II's mission to Ireland, the English kings turned more and more to European affairs and neglected the lordship of Ireland. The result was that from 1400 the colony declined very rapidly because the kings failed to provide viceroys with enough men and money to defend it. Later, the civil war in England, known as the Wars of the Roses, caused them to neglect Ireland even more. Ireland fell more and more under the power of the three great Earls: the Earl of Ormond, the Earl of Desmond and the Earl of Kildare.

The Earldom of Ormond

The Earls of Ormond, the Butlers, ruled over all Kilkenny and Tipperary, and had their seat at Kilkenny. The Earl was feudal lord of the English families, Graces, Purcells and others and he claimed to be lord also of the Gaelic rulers, Mac Giolla Phádraig of Ossory, O'Carroll of Ely, O'Kennedy of Ormond and lesser rulers. James, fourth Earl of Ormond (1408–52) was the greatest lord in the Ireland of his day. According to the Irish annalist, he was 'the best captain of the English nation that ever was in Ireland'. He was known as the White Earl. He was a gallant and cultured man and Kilkenny, his capital, was a great centre of Anglo-Irish culture. The White Earl was viceroy on a number of occasions. He was the leader of the great nobles who hated interference in Irish affairs by the king's English officials and by his supporters in Ireland. He carried on a great feud with the king's officers and especially with his great enemy, Talbot, who held office as viceroy for a period. Led by the White Earl, the great lords succeeded from about 1450 in dominating the Irish parliament and dividing out the offices of government among themselves. However, Ormond never became as gaelicized as the Geraldines and maintained a closer connection with England. The White Earl died in 1452 and he was succeeded by his son, James, who married an English noblewoman. He was created Earl of Wiltshire and he and his successors lived mostly in England. The leadership of the great lords then passed to the Earls of Desmond.

Ormond Castle, Carrick-on-Suir, one of the castles of the Butlers of Ormond.

The ruins of Terryglass Castle, Co. Tipperary, another centre of Butler power.

The Earldom of Desmond

The Earls of Desmond extended their sway over the whole of Kerry, Cork and Limerick and even over the western half of Waterford. The Earl of Desmond had his seat at Tralee and he was the feudal lord of a great number of ruling houses both Gaelic and Norman. The various branches of the MacCarthys—MacCarthy More, MacCarthy Reagh and MacCarthy of Muskerry—and the O'Sullivans of West Cork and Kerry recognized him as their lord and paid him head-rents. The junior branches of the Geraldines of Munster (the FitzGeralds of the Decies, the Knight of Glin, the Knight of Kerry), the Barrys of Barrymore and Buttevant, the Roches of Fermoy and the other Norman families recognized him as their feudal lord. In addition, the Earl of Desmond held the four great ports of Munster—Cork, Youghal, Tralee and Limerick. Under James, 6th Earl of Desmond (1420–62), Desmond was in fact a small kingdom. James was fostered among the Irish, ruled his earldom by Gaelic and feudal custom, brought in MacSheehy as the captain of his gallowglasses, and retained Ó Dálaigh as his hereditary poet. In a later account we read of an Earl of Desmond:

The ruins of the great castle at Askeaton, Co. Limerick, which was partly rebuilt by James, Earl of Desmond.

In all three cities, Waterford, Cork and Limerick, the Earl of Desmond has lordships and vassals. He has dominions also among the wild tribes; he has lords and knights upon his estates who pay him tribute . . . He has ten castles of his own, some of which are strong and well-built, especially one named Dungarvan . . . He keeps better justice throughout his dominions than any chief in Ireland. Robbers and homicides find no mercy and are executed out of hand. His people are in high order and discipline.

James was a great builder of castles and he built or rebuilt the great castles of Imokilly, Askeaton and Connells.

The Earldom of Kildare

The Earl of Kildare was later to become the most powerful of all the great Norman lords but until about 1470 Kildare was the weakest of all the great lords. However, his vast estates lay on the borders of the Pale and he was in a position to dominate it. He was the feudal lord of more than half the Pale. He exercised and extended his authority over the ruling families, Gaelic and English in the counties Kildare, Carlow, Wicklow, Leix and Offaly. He claimed rents of MacMurrough, O'Byrne, O'Toole, O'Connor of Offaly and the Great Earl, who succeeded to his estates in 1477 became the greatest Norman lord in Ireland.

Richard, Duke of York, in Ireland

After 1435, when England was under the rule of the weak king, Henry VI of Lancaster, two parties emerged among the great English nobles: those who wished to continue the war with France and those who wished to make peace. In 1444, the king married a French wife, Margaret of Anjou, and the party in favour of peace was in power. The Duke of Gloucester was the leader of the opposition party and, if the king had no heir by his new marriage, Gloucester was heir to the throne. However, Gloucester was murdered in mysterious circumstances in 1447 and Richard, Duke of York, became next heir to the throne. York was a handsome man of thirty-six who possessed huge estates in England. In Ireland he was heir to the earldom of Ulster and the lordships of Leix, Trim and Connacht. York had powerful connections amongst the English nobility and he had served with distinction in the French wars. In 1447, York was appointed viceroy in Ireland. He was an experienced soldier and he had wide interests in Ireland and so was naturally suitable for his new post. However, the king and his supporters feared York, and hoped his position in Ireland would keep him busy and prevent him interfering too much

Muckross Abbey, near Killarney, Co. Kerry. It was founded for the Franciscans in 1448 by Donal MacCarthy. It is the burial place of many famous Munstermen, including Aodhagán Ó Rathaile, the great Munster poet.

in England. But York was a clever politician and he built up powerful support for himself in Ireland.

York as Viceroy

York arrived in Ireland in 1449, accompanied by his beautiful wife, Cecily Neville, and he landed at Howth with great pomp and ceremony. He was warmly welcomed by the great nobles of Ireland who dearly loved a prince of the royal blood. He called out the forces of the colony and marched into Ulster. The Gaelic rulers of the north, including the great O'Neill himself, submitted to him and did him homage. Later, the midland rulers and the Earl of Desmond submitted. He then turned against the rebellious Gaelic rulers of Leinster and O'Byrne and MacMurrough soon submitted to him. This was followed by the submission of a long list of Gaelic rulers. As one great historian puts it, 'it became the thing to march in imposingly with troops and visit this gallant deputy of the king, who, the Irish thought, was himself every inch a King'. One English observer was so hopeful that he wrote '. . . with the might of Jesus ere twelve months come to an end the wildest Irishman in Ireland shall be sworn English'. But as usual the documents of submission, signed by the Gaelic rulers, men who could be conquered only by the sword, were not worth the paper they were written on.

The Norman lords of Ireland took York more seriously. There were great scenes of rejoicing in Dublin in October 1449 when York's beautiful wife gave birth to a son. The

A drawing of one of the Burkes of Connacht from an illustrated genealogy preserved in Trinity College, Dublin.

Earls of Desmond and Ormond stood as sponsors for the child. York held a great council in autumn 1449 which forbade abuses such as coign and livery and the keeping of private armies and a number of rules were passed providing for the defence too of the colony. Early in 1450, York summoned a parliament to meet at Drogheda to discuss his financial position. He had not been paid the money promised him from England for the wages and upkeep of his army. He received some money from the parliament but York's attention was now on England. Things in England were moving rapidly towards disorder and civil war and York's claim to the throne was receiving some support in England. By now York had won the support and firm loyalty of the great lords of Ireland, and with Ireland firmly in his grasp, he left Ormond as his deputy, and returned to England.

York's Second Visit to Ireland

In 1455, the Wars of the Roses began and, at the battle of St Albans, York defeated his enemies, the house of Lancaster. York's supporters were dominant until 1458 but in 1459 York and his followers were defeated at Ludford Bridge. York fled to Ireland where the great lords were his supporters and his son, the later Edward IV, fled to France. Both of them were declared traitors. York was welcomed like a messiah by the lords of Ireland and there were great scenes of rejoicing when he arrived. He summoned a parliament which met in Drogheda in 1460. The parliament made it high treason to plot against York. It declared that Ireland was independent of all English laws, being subject only to the laws passed and proclaimed by her own parliament. This meant that Ireland was independent except for the fact that the king of England was also lord of Ireland. The parliament declared that Ireland was to have a separate coinage of her own and it ordered that mints be set up in Dublin and Trim. Three varieties of coin were struck: a silver 'Ireland' valued at a penny sterling, a 'Patrick' valued at one-eighth of an 'Ireland' and a groat, valued at four pence. The parliament also formed a force of archers for the defence of the colony and for York.

One of the last acts of this parliament permitted all who wished to absent themselves from Ireland and go to England to support York in the Wars of the Roses. In the spring of 1460, Warwick, York's nephew, sailed into Waterford, with a fleet of twenty-six ships and held a conference with York. Shortly afterwards, Warwick landed in Kent and marched northwards, defeating the Lancastrians as he went and he captured the king at Northampton. As soon as York heard the news of this victory, he appointed the Earl of Kildare as his deputy and sailed for England. However, York was slain in battle but his son, Edward IV, was crowned king of England in 1461.

The great lords of Ireland made good use of the Wars of the Roses, and won legislative independence for the Irish parliament. This meant that Ireland was bound only by laws passed and approved by the Irish parliament. And these same great lords dominated the Irish parliament and made use of it to strengthen themselves.

The official seal of the City of Dublin, 1459.

Thomas, Seventh Earl of Desmond

Thomas became Earl of Desmond in 1462. He was, according to an Irish annalist, 'the most illustrious of his tribe in Ireland in his time for his comeliness and stature, for his hospitality, and chivalry, for his charity and humanity to the poor . . .'

His great enemies were the Butlers who alone of the Irish nobility supported the House of Lancaster. They suffered with the fall of Lancaster and James, Earl of Ormond, was executed by Edward IV in 1461 for supporting the Lancastrians. In 1462, the Butlers attempted to revive their fortunes in Ireland but they were defeated by the Earl of Desmond with great slaughter at the battle of Pilltown, near Carrick-on-Suir. Edmund MacRichard Butler was captured in battle and ransomed himself by handing over to Desmond a valuable Irish manuscript. The victory at Pilltown made Desmond the most powerful man in Ireland and in 1463 Edward IV appointed him viceroy. Desmond had acts passed enabling Cork, Youghal, Waterford and Limerick to trade with the Gaelic people. He made provision for the protection of the Pale. He was himself a cultured man learned in Irish, English and Latin and he was a patron of the poets.

He attempted to found a university at Drogheda but unfortunately the attempt came to nothing. Through his connections with the Anglo-Irish nobility and the Gaelic rulers, Desmond exercised very wide authority. However, he had many enemies in Ireland. Some thought him too fond of the Gaelic rulers and of Gaelic customs. Some suspected that he wished to make himself king of Ireland. In 1467 he was dismissed from his post as viceroy and Sir John Tiptoft, an English nobleman, known as 'the Butcher' was appointed in his place.

Shortly after his arrival in Ireland, Tiptoft had the Earls of Desmond and Kildare attainted of 'horrible treasons and felonies.' When Desmond came to Drogheda to answer the charges made against him, he was taken in treachery and beheaded. All Ireland was shocked by this ugly deed. He was according to one writer 'slain by the swords of the wicked or shall I say rather made a martyr of Christ.' Kildare eventually escaped to England where he was pardoned by the king and restored. Meanwhile, Garret of Desmond, the murdered Earl's brother, wreaked vengeance on the colony. He marched into Meath with thousands of gallowglasses and ravaged and destroyed it. He ravaged Tipperary and burned Fethard. Soon all the south was in a state of war and confusion and O'Neill and his supporters were raiding the Pale from the north. James, the Earl's son, rose in rebellion and swore that he and his successors would never attend parliament or enter a royal walled town except at their own pleasure. James went more Irish than his father. He married Margaret, a daughter of O'Brien and bound himself closely in alliance with the Gaelic rulers. The great earldom of Desmond was lost to English loyalty until the days of Elizabeth.

Tiptoft's failure showed the real difficulty of any settlement of Ireland. The reconquest of Ireland could only be achieved by the expenditure of huge sums of money and greater military forces than the king of England could provide. The only alternative was to give the government of Ireland to the great Anglo-Irish lords who, because of their great power and close connections with the Gaelic rulers, could govern Ireland more effectively than any Englishman. From this time forward, then, Ireland was governed by the great nobles of Ireland, particularly the Earls of Kildare.

The Ballymacasey Cross. A processional cross made for Cornelius O'Connor of Kerry in 1479.

The Rise of Kildare

After the murder of the Earl of Desmond, the Geraldines of Munster took little interest in the affairs of the government. The Earl of Ormond was a permanent absentee in England. This, and the weakness of the English crown, paved the way for the rise of the House of Kildare. After the departure of Tiptoft, Thomas, seventh Earl of Kildare, held the office of viceroy almost continuously. Kildare gradually built up his strength making use of the parliament to pass laws which suited himself. In 1474, for example, the parliament established the Guild of St George a body of 200 well-armed troops, paid for by the state to defend the Pale; but, in practice, it was almost a private army for the Earl of Kildare. Thomas died in 1477 and he was succeeded by his son, Garret More, the Great Earl of Kildare.

The Great Earl of Kildare

Garret More became Earl of Kildare on the death of his father in 1477. He was twenty-one when he succeeded to the earldom and to the vast estates of his family, estates which he himself busily extended during his lifetime. He drew rents from Kildare, Carlow, Wicklow, Leix, Offaly and from further afield. His estates lay along the western and south-western borders of the Pale, within easy reach of Dublin and he himself was feudal lord of a great portion of the Pale. His great castle of Maynooth lay within fifteen miles of the capital. He was ideally placed, then, to dominate the government in Dublin. Immediately on the death of his father he was elected viceroy by the Irish council. The king attempted to deprive him of his office and sent over Lord Grey as viceroy in his stead. But Garret More and his supporters defied Grey. They garrisoned Dublin Castle, broke down the bridge and refused him admittance. Grey returned to England and Garret More was restored as viceroy.

The power of Garret More did not depend only on his

being viceroy. He strengthened and fortified himself at every opportunity by marriage-alliances with the great nobles, Gaelic and Norman. His sister, Eleanor, was married to Conn Mór, the eldest son of Henry O'Neill, lord of Tyrone, and his daughter Alice was married to Conn Bacach O'Neill. In this way, the two greatest families in Ireland were united by marriage. Of his daughters, one was married to Sir Piers Rua Butler, the head of the Butlers in Ireland; another to Dónal MacCarthy Reagh, a third to Ulick Burke of Clanrickarde, and a fourth to O'Carroll, lord of Ely. O'Donnell entered into a military alliance with him which remained unbroken until his death. A great lord in his own right, the king's representative in Ireland and the head of a powerful web of alliances, Garret More was all but king of Ireland until his death in 1513. Every year his forces were on the march throughout Ireland, supporting his allies and curbing his enemies. He imposed coign and livery and quartered his gallowglasses on the loyal citizens of the Pale. He was an open supporter of the House of York and he could defy, and did defy, the king himself. Even when Henry VII of Lancaster became king he could not remove Garret More who was openly disloyal to him.

The De Burgo-O'Malley Chalice. A silver gilt chalice made in 1494 for Thomas de Burgo and Grainne O'Malley. It was probably made in Galway.

Lambert Simnel

On Bosworth field in 1485, Richard III, the last English king of the House of York fell, and Henry Tudor of the House of Lancaster became king as Henry VII. Though Garret More was a Yorkist, Henry VII did not remove him but continued him as viceroy. In 1487, a boy of ten years of age claiming to be Edward, Earl of Warwick and Yorkist heir to the English crown was brought to Dublin. The lords of Ireland, including Garret More and the Earl of Desmond, and the archbishops of Armagh and Dublin accepted him and declared their support for him. The Duchess of Burgundy, the aunt of the real Edward of Warwick sent 2,000 German mercenaries to Ireland to support him and he was crowned king as Edward VI in Dublin. The lad was in fact an impostor called Lambert Simnel. Only the city of Waterford and the Butler lands stood out for Henry VII. In June 1487, Simnel and his supporters landed in England but they were defeated in battle at Stoke. Lambert Simnel was captured in the battle and was made a kitchen-boy by Henry VII. Henry forgave Garret More and continued him in office as viceroy. He had no other choice because Garret More was too powerful a man to dislodge. Henry merely sent an envoy over to Ireland where, after much hesitation, the lords of Ireland took an oath of loyalty to Henry and in return they received a full pardon.

Perkin Warbeck

Late in 1491, a young man of seventeen, who claimed to be Richard, son of Edward IV and rightful Yorkist heir to the crown of England, arrived in Cork from Lisbon. The great lords of the south, led by the Earl of Desmond and by the archbishop of Cashel and the bishop of Waterford accepted him as Prince Richard and declared their support for him. It seems that he received very little support from Garret More. The young man was in fact an impostor whose real name was Perkin Warbeck. After a brief stay he left Ireland and did not return until 1495.

Henry VII, king of England and the first of the Tudor dynasty. From a portrait by an unknown Flemish artist. In his hand, Henry holds the red rose of Lancaster.

Sir Edward Poynings as Viceroy, 1494–96

In 1494, Henry VII deprived Garret More of his office as viceroy and sent over in his place an English knight, Sir Edward Poynings, with orders to reduce Ireland 'to whole and perfect obedience.' He was accompanied by a force of 1,000 men including archers, mounted and on foot, and gunners. Poynings' first act was to lead an expedition against the northern rulers, O'Hanlon and Magennis. This expedition went badly and Garret More was suspected of being in league with the enemy. Poynings then summoned a parliament at Drogheda in December 1494.

Poynings' Parliament, 1494

The first act of this parliament was to attaint Garret More 'for treason and rebellion, taking coign and livery . . . inciting Irish enemies and English rebels to make war against the king and his deputy . . .' Garret More was arrested in Dublin early in 1495, sent to England and lodged as a prisoner in the Tower of London. The parliament then passed a number of important acts. It declared that the chief officers of the government should hold office only during the king's pleasure and not for life as before. It declared null and void the right of the great lords to appoint a viceroy in the case of a sudden vacancy, and it dissolved the Guild of St George. All these acts were directed against the Earl of Kildare and his supporters who dominated the government of Ireland. The most famous act passed was the act known as Poynings' Law. According to this act parliament could meet in Ireland only with the king's permission and only after the king and his council in England had been informed of the acts which were to be passed and had approved of them. The main purpose of this act was to prevent the Irish parliament recognizing rival claimants to the throne or pretenders such as Simnel and Warbeck.

Other acts were passed for the better government and protection of the Pale. All laws passed in England for the public good in the time of the king and his predecessors were declared binding in Ireland. The Statutes of Kilkenny were re-enacted but the section forbidding the speaking of Irish was omitted. The exaction of coign and livery was forbidden and orders were given that a double ditch, six feet high, be built around the Pale to protect it.

The Restoration of Garret More

Henry VII soon found that he could not govern Ireland without Garret More for Poynings had few successes against the Irish. Perkin Warbeck landed in Cork in 1495 and soon besieged Waterford which was relieved by Poynings. Henry decided to restore Garret More as viceroy, the charge of treason was dropped and he was released from the Tower. The *Book of Howth* has the story of his interview with Henry after his release. The bishop of Meath attacked Garret More and said: 'All Ireland cannot rule yonder gentleman.' The king replied: 'Then he is fit to rule all Ireland seeing that all Ireland cannot rule him.' Henry then granted a general pardon to all those who had supported Perkin Warbeck, remarking sarcastically: 'They will crown apes next.' The unfortunate Perkin Warbeck came to a bad end. He arrived again in Cork in 1497 but he received little support and he tried his luck in England. At last he surrendered and in 1499 he was executed at Tyburn.

Henry VIII, king of England 1509–1547. From a portrait by Hans Holbein.

The Later Years of Garret More 1496–1513

Garret More remained the most powerful man in Ireland until his death. Year after year he went on great hostings into Ulster, Connacht and Desmond, playing his part in the continuous warfare and border-struggles of the great lords of Ireland. Garret More combined the king's interest and his own. Henry VII left him free to do much as he pleased. In 1503, the king summoned him to London and he returned laden with honours, Garret's greatest victory was won at Knocktoe in 1504. Ulick Burke of Clanrickarde, who was married to Garrett More's daughter, ill-treated her. He also occupied the city of Galway and made war on O'Kelly of Uí Maine. O'Kelly called for aid on Garret More, who marched into Connacht with his allies, O'Neill, O'Donnell, the lords of the Pale and others. Ulick Burke had the support of O'Brien and the Gaelic rulers of Ormond but he was utterly defeated.

Garret More had the power to sweep the English forces out of Ireland, wipe out the tiny colony, and make himself king of Ireland. He never did. The Old English always retained some loyalty for the Crown and Garret More followed the traditions of his class. Even though he was a Yorkist to the bone, he

The highly carved and ornamented tomb of Piers Butler at Kilcooley Abbey, Co. Tipperary. The panels depict the apostles and are done in the Irish style.

served the Lancastrian kings well and loyally. And Garret knew that it would be as difficult for him to subdue the great lords of Ireland as it would be for the king of England himself. He was content to be the most powerful man in Ireland, Ireland's uncrowned king. In 1509, the young and ambitious Henry VIII succeeded to the throne of England. With Henry, the English crown recovered greater strength than it had had for a hundred years and now at last the kings of England had the power and the money to begin the reconquest of Ireland. In the early years of his reign, Henry was much taken up with European politics and he paid little attention to Ireland. Garret More was retained as viceroy until his death from gunshot wounds received in battle against O'More of Leix in 1513. He was according to one writer 'a warrior incomparable, a man hardly able to rule himself when moved to anger yet not so sharp as short-tempered, being easily displeased and sooner appeased . . .' He handed on to his son, Garret Óg, his great estates and high prestige. Garret Óg became viceroy and for another twenty years the House of Kildare dominated Ireland. However, the old world of great and gallant lords, ruling like sovereigns, passed away with the death of Garret More. The new and powerful rulers of England would have no powerful lords as rivals to their authority. Soon, the Tudor reconquest of Ireland began and the House of Kildare, the greatest family in Ireland was the first to fall.

Things to Do

1. James Earl of Desmond, was a great castle-builder and so were many other great lords. Make a list of the castles in your neighbourhood and find out as much as you can about them.
2. What was the attitude of the great lords of Ireland to the king? Why did the English kings allow them to be so independent?
3. Account for the great power of Garret More. Why did he never attempt to make himself king of Ireland?

Books to Read or Consult

Lord Dunboyne, *Butler Family History*, Kilkenny 1968.

K. M. Lanigan, *Kilkenny Castle*, Kilkenny 1968.

Brian Fitzgerald, *The Geraldines*, London 1951.

D. Bryan, Gerald Fitzgerald, *The Great Earl of Kildare*, Dublin 1933.

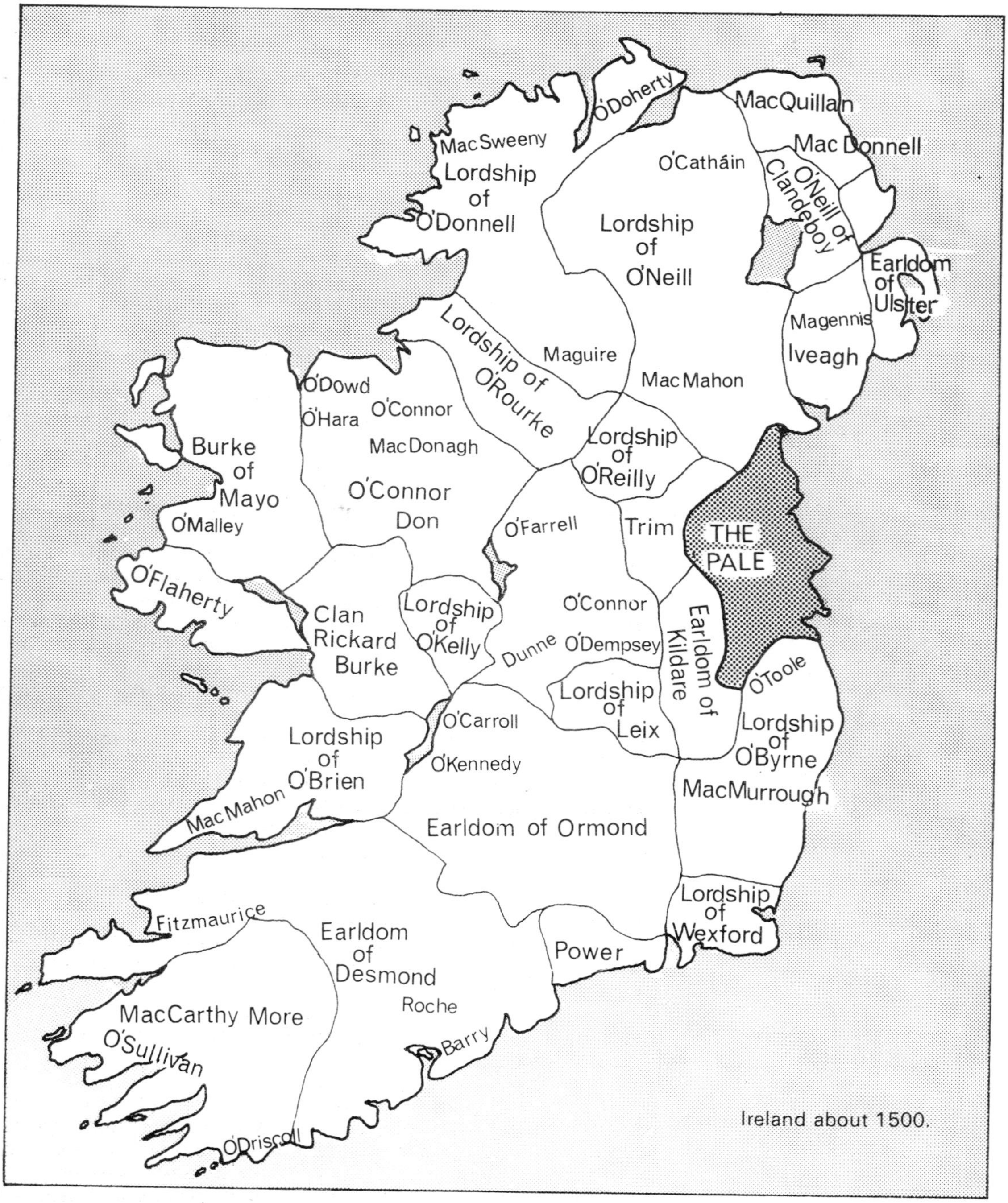

O'Doherty
MacQuillan
Mac Donnell
O'Catháin
O'Neill of Clandeboy
MacSweeny
Lordship of O'Donnell
Lordship of O'Neill
Earldom of Ulster
Magennis
Iveagh
Lordship of O'Rourke
Maguire
MacMahon
O'Dowd
O'Hara
O'Connor
MacDonagh
Burke of Mayo
O'Connor Don
Lordship of O'Reilly
O'Malley
O'Farrell
Trim
THE PALE
O'Flaherty
Clan Rickard Burke
Lordship of O'Kelly
O'Connor
Dunne
O'Dempsey
Earldom of Kildare
O'Toole
Lordship of Leix
O'Carroll
Lordship of O'Brien
O'Kennedy
Lordship of O'Byrne
MacMurrough
MacMahon
Earldom of Ormond
Lordship of Wexford
Fitzmaurice
Earldom of Desmond
Power
Roche
MacCarthy More
O'Sullivan
Barry
O'Driscoll
Ireland about 1500.

Glossary

absentee: a person not present especially a landlord who lives away from his estates and tenants.
adaptive: easily changed or made suitable to a new way of life or work.
annalist: a person who writes books of annals, a year-by-year account of events. The great Irish books of annals are: *Annals of Ulster, Annals of Inisfallen, Annals of Tigernach, Annals of Clonmacnoise, Chronicon Scotorum, Annals of Boyle, Annals of Connacht* and, the best known of all, *Annals of the Four Masters*.
Antipodes: places directly opposite one another, especially the parts of the world directly on the opposite side of the globe from us.
belfries: towers or spires on which bells are hung, especially in churches.
Brehon laws: the ancient native laws of Ireland which were written down and preserved by the brehons or men learned in the law.
bubonic plague: a highly contagious sickness which spread rapidly among the people. The sickness caused inflamed swelling in the groin and armpits and few people survived it.
burgess: a citizen of a town or city which had a charter of freedom.
canonical hours: according to the law of the Church, the clergy have to recite the Psalms and other prayers and parts of the Scripture at certain fixed hours in the day. These are known as the canonical hours.
charter: a written grant of rights and privileges, usually granted by a king or ruler.
colonists: persons who settle in a new country and occupy lands there. They often drove out the native people or else treated them badly. The area settled by the colonists is called a colony.
commentaries: explanations or notes written upon a text. Commentaries on the Scripture are notes which explain the meaning of the Scriptures.
commissioned: a person who is given power to act in another person's name is said to be commissioned.
confederacy: a league or alliance of different rulers or powers.
contingent: a force of soldiers contributed to form part of an army.
copper deposits: copper ore lying beneath the ground.
crozier: the pastoral staff borne by a bishop or abbot which may still be seen in solemn church ceremonies.
demesne: the part of the landlord's estate which he reserves for his own use.
deposed: removed from office, especially dethroned.
devastation: laying waste, ravaging or plundering.
domestic: concerning the home, the household and family affairs.
engrossed: a person is engrossed in something when all his attention is taken up by it.
entrenched: surrounded by trenches or defences.
episcopal: relating to a bishop. An episcopal Church is a Church ruled by bishops.
expenditure: the spending of money.
Exchequer: the government department which takes care of money matters. Nowadays we would call it the Department of Finance.
faction fighting: fights with sticks and cudgels which took place in Ireland between groups of men from different parishes or areas. They continued down to the nineteenth century and usually took place at fairs and outings.

forays: raids, especially raids made into enemy territory.

Gaelicized: to become Gaelicized is to become Irish. When the Normans turned over to the Irish language and the Irish way of life we say they became Gaelicized.

gallowglass: a professional soldier from the Western Isles of Scotland. Many gallowglasses founded families of great distinction in Ireland: MacAlister, MacRory, MacSweeny, MacCabe, MacSheehy (now Sheehy) and several others.

genealogy: a pedigree or account of a man's descent which lists his father, grandfather, great-grandfather and so on.

gossipred: the relationship made when one stands sponsor for another person's child at baptism. In Ireland, this was a very sacred relationship.

homicide: the killing of a human being.

hostage: a person who is handed over to another as a pledge. A king gave hostages to another king as a pledge that he would do what he promised. If he failed to do so, the hostages could be executed.

immigrants: persons who come as settlers into a foreign country.

inaugurate: Irish kings were inaugurated or granted the office of kingship in a solemn ceremony.

infield: the land lying close to the house.

impostor: a person who passes himself off as somebody else; a pretender.

landlord: a person who owns lands or property and receives rent from tenants to whom he lets land or property.

legislative independence: the right of a country to make its own law without interference from another country.

mercenaries: professional soldiers who fight for pay.

Merovingian: the name given to a succession of French kings who were very weak rulers. They were known as the 'Do Nothing' kings.

military opposition: opposition by armed forces.

monasticism: the practice of establishing monasteries and having communities of monks living together under a rule.

negotiations: discussions with a view to coming to an agreement.

palisade: a fence of strong wooden stakes.

pallium: woollen vestments worn by the pope and archbishops. The pallium is conferred by the pope on archbishops as a sign of their office.

papal legate: the pope's personal representative abroad. Nowadays we would call him the papal nuncio.

professional soldier: a man who makes his living by being a soldier. In the Middle Ages many professional soldiers were mercenaries.

quarters: a place where soldiers are lodged.

reconquest: conquering for a second time. By the end of the Middle Ages the Norman conquest of Ireland had failed and so a reconquest was necessary, that is, Ireland had to be conquered again.

reeve: the chief officer in the government of a town; a mayor.

refugee: a person who has to flee from his home or country because of danger or persecution.

reinforcements: additional troops brought up to add to the strength of an army.

renovated: renewed, repaired or rebuilt.

retinue: a group of people who are in attendance on an important person.

satire: a composition in verse or prose written to mock or ridicule a person.

scroll: a design with flowing lines like a roll of parchment or paper.

simony: the buying or selling of offices in the Church.

status: a person's standing in life.

tenant: a person who occupies land or property under a landlord.

timpanist: a person who plays an instrument like a drum or *bodhrán*.

treason: disloyalty to one's king or country. It was high treason for a subject to attempt to bring about the king's death or to make war on the king.

tribute: money or goods paid by one king or country to another as a sign of submission.

tuath: a petty Irish kingdom in ancient times. There were 150 or more *tuatha* in Ireland.

usury: the charging of an unjustly high rate of interest on money lent.

variegated: of different colours.

Viking sagas: historical tales preserved by the Vikings about their voyages, wars and settlements.

wars of succession: wars fought for the kingship of a country between rival claimants.

Significant Dates

6000 B.C. (about) The first evidence of man in Ireland.
2000 B.C. (about) The first metal-workers in Ireland.
700–600 B.C. The Celts conquer the greater part of Europe.
600 B.C. (about) The Celts arrive in Ireland and Britain.
490 A.D. (about) St Enna founds his monastery on Aran.
550 (about) St Ciaran founds Clonmacnoise.
563 St Columcille goes on his mission to Scotland.
590 St Columbanus begins his mission to the continent.
650 (about) The writing of the *Book of Durrow*, the earliest of the great Irish illuminated manuscripts.
795 The first Viking raids on Ireland.
841 The Vikings found Dublin.
980 The defeat of the Vikings at the Battle of Tara.
1005 Brian becomes high king of Ireland.
1014 The battle of Clontarf.
1066 The Normans invade England.
1169 The Normans invade Ireland.
1171 Henry II visits Ireland.
1175 The treaty of Windsor.
1185 Prince John visits Ireland.
1200 (about) The first great stone castles built in Ireland.
1235 The Normans invade Connacht.
1260 The battle of Down.
1261 The battle of Callann.
1315–18 The Bruce invasion of Ireland.
1318 Edward Bruce slain at Faughart.
1333 Ulster lost by the Normans.
1348 The Black Death appears in Ireland.
1366 The Statutes of Kilkenny.
1394 The first visit of Richard II to Ireland.
1399 Richard II again visits Ireland.
1449 Richard, Duke of York, comes as Viceroy to Ireland.
1467 Thomas, Earl of Desmond, executed by Tiptoft.
1477 Garret More becomes Earl of Kildare.
1494 Poynings' Law.
1513 The death of Garret More.

Acknowledgments

Grateful acknowledgment is made to the following for assistance in selection of illustrations and for permission to reproduce pictures in this book.
National Museum of Ireland; Commissioners of Public Works in Ireland; National Library of Ireland; An tAthair Tomás Ó Fiaich; Royal Irish Academy; Board of Trinity College, Dublin; Bord Fáilte Éireann; Department of Posts and Telegraphs; Cork Public Museum; Cultural Relations Committee, Department of External Affairs; Universitetets Oldsaksamling, Oslo; British Museum, London; Bodleian Library, Oxford; National Portrait Gallery, London; City of Norwich Museums; Courtauld Institute of Art and the Dean and Chapter of Lichfield Cathedral; City of Liverpool Museums; County Borough of Reading Museum and Art Galleries; National Museum of Antiquities of Scotland; Scottish National Portrait Gallery; Glasgow Museums and Art Galleries; Landesmuseum, Bonn; Landesmuseum, Stuttgart; Staatliche Museen zu Berlin; Musée des Antiquités Nationales, Paris; Museo Capitolino, Rome.